INTERNATIONAL TRADE IN
BUSINESS SERVICES

The American Enterprise Institute
Trade in Services Series

COMPETING IN A CHANGING WORLD ECONOMY PROJECT

Deregulation and Globalization: Liberalizing International Trade in Air Services — *Daniel M. Kasper*

Global Competition in Financial Services: Market Structure, Protection, and Trade Liberalization — *Ingo Walter*

International Trade in Business Services: Accounting, Advertising, Law, and Management Consulting — *Thierry J. Noyelle and Anna B. Dutka*

International Trade in Construction, Design, and Engineering Services — *James R. Lee and David Walters*

International Trade in Films and Television Programs — *Steven S. Wildman and Stephen E. Siwek*

International Trade in Ocean Shipping Services: The United States and the World — *Lawrence J. White*

When Countries Talk: International Trade in Telecommunications Services — *Jonathan David Aronson and Peter F. Cowhey*

International Trade in Services: An Overview and Blueprint for Negotiations — *Geza Feketekuty*

International Trade in Business Services

Accounting, Advertising, Law, and Management Consulting

Thierry J. Noyelle
Anna B. Dutka

An American Enterprise Institute/Ballinger Publication

Ballinger Publishing Company, Cambridge, Massachusetts
A Subsidiary of Harper & Row, Publishers, Inc.

"American Enterprise Institute" and ⟨🐾⟩ are registered service marks of the American Enterprise Institute for Public Policy Research.

International Standard Book Number: 0-88730-237-8

Library of Congress Catalog Card Number: 87-30819

Printed in the United States of America.

Library of Congress Cataloging-in-Publication Data

Noyelle, Thierry J.
  International trade in business services: accounting, advertising, law, and management consulting / Thierry J. Noyelle, Anna B. Dutka.
  p.   cm. — (American Enterprise Institute series on trade in services)
    "An American Enterprise Institute/Ballinger publication."
    "Developed under a contract from the American Enterprise Institute (AEI) as part of the Institute's 'Competing in a Changing World Economy Project' "—Verso of t.p.
    Includes index.
    ISBN 0-88730-237-8
  1. Business consultants.   2. Lawyers.   3. Accountants.   4. Advertising.   5. Service industries.   6. International trade.
I. Dutka, Anna B.   II. American Enterprise Institute for Public Policy Research.
III. Title.   IV. Title: Business services.   V. Series.
HD69.C6N68   1988
382'.45—dc19   87-30819
                                                                                              CIP

CONTENTS

LIST OF TABLES

EDITOR'S FOREWORD

The American Enterprise Institute's *Trade in Services Series* represents an important step toward creating the policy alternatives necessary to enhance the international competitiveness of American services.

The series is part of a larger, continuing AEI project, *Competing in a Changing World Economy*. Launched in 1983, this project has produced a wealth of publications, seminars, and conferences, analyzing the most significant policy challenges confronting U.S. policymakers in the areas of international trade and finance, science and technology policy, and human capital development.

Early in the project, we concluded that the United States would be successful in its drive to initiate a new round of trade negotiations with the other major trading nations, under the auspices of the General Agreement on Tariffs and Trade (GATT). We also chose to concentrate our resources on the new issues that would be placed on the table in that round: trade in services, intellectual property, and trade-related investment. In September 1986, at Punta del Este, Uruguay, the United States and the other members of GATT did indeed reach an agreement to launch a new multilateral round of trade negotiations, the Uruguay Round. Trade in services, along with intellectual property and investment issues, was included on the agenda. Hence, over the next several years negotiators in Geneva and top policy officials in all the major trading nations will face the formidable task of forging trading rules for these new issues.

In the area of services, a number of countries, including the United States, have produced individual, national studies of service trade liberalization. Yet government and private-sector officials agree that these studies are only a first step, and that substantial research remains to be done in key service sectors before major policy questions can be answered regarding a new service trade regime.

Designed to fill this policy gap, *Trade in Services* brings together eleven outstanding writers who have committed their expertise to analyzing the seven key service sector industries:

- Aviation—Daniel M. Kasper, Harbridge House

- Banking—Ingo Walter, Graduate School of Business Administration, New York University

- Construction—James R. Lee, American University, and David Walters, Staff Economist, Office of the U.S. Trade Representative

- Professional services—Thierry J. Noyelle and Anna B. Dutka, Conservation of Human Resources, Columbia University

- Shipping—Lawrence J. White, Member, Federal Home Loan Bank Board, on leave from the Graduate School of Business Administration, New York University

- Telecommunications: Information and Data Processing— Jonathan David Aronson, School of International Relations, University of Southern California, and Peter F. Cowhey, Department of Political Science, University of California at San Diego

- Telecommunications: Motion Pictures, Television, and Prerecorded Entertainment—Steven S. Wildman and Stephen E. Siwek, Economists Incorporated

In addition, Geza Feketekuty, of the Office of the U.S. Trade Representative, has written an overview volume for the series.

All of the books in the series embody two main goals: first, to analyze the dynamics of international competition for each of the seven industries, identifying existing and potential barriers to trade; and second, to formulate and assess policy approaches for opening service markets through an umbrella service agreement and subsequent individual sector agreements in GATT.

A related goal is to disseminate the results of our research through conferences and seminars, televised forums, and a variety of publication formats. We aim to make our findings known to government officials, trade experts, the business and financial communities, and concerned members of the public. To that end, during 1987 we convened major conferences in London, Geneva, and Washington, and in early 1988 the team of authors traveled to Tokyo and Singapore. Thus, as with all AEI projects, we have sought to ensure that the studies not only make a significant contribution to scholarship but also become an important factor in the decision making and negotiating processes.

In addition to the authors, who have produced outstanding books, we would like to thank John H. Jackson, Hessel E. Yntema Professor of Law at the University of Michigan, and Gardner Patterson, who for many years served in the GATT Secretariat. Both of these men provided invaluable help and guidance as advisers to the project.

—*Claude E. Barfield*
Coordinator
Competing in a Changing World Economy

FOREWORD

A quarter of a century has passed since the Conservation of Human Resources Project (CHR) at Columbia University first detected that important changes were occurring in the United States and other advanced economies as a result of steady and continuing increases in the production of services relative to manufacturing. From that day on, a considerable part of CHR's research has been directed to deepening its understanding of the shift to services in developed economies.

One of CHR's earliest inquiries explored the strategic role that "producer services" played in the expansion of the service sector (Harry Greenfield, *Manpower and the Growth of Producer Services*, 1966). In an article summarizing CHR's research in the late 1970s ("The Service Sector of the U.S. Economy," *Scientific American*, March 1981), Eli Ginzberg and George Vojta calculated that "business services"—defined as the services provided to business enterprises and individuals by freestanding firms such as banking, legal, accounting, management consulting, advertising, marketing, communications, and others—accounted for approximately the same net contribution to the gross national product as did the manufacturing sector, each falling in the 20 to 25 percent range.

This last point is a sharp reminder of the relative neglect of services in general, and business services in particular, in the allocation of resources to data gathering, economic analysis, and policy explorations affecting the contemporary U.S. economy. More aware than most of the serious consequences of this underinvestment in the study of services, CHR was pleased when asked by the American Enterprise Institute (AEI) to participate in its multipronged effort to assist the Office of the U.S. Trade Representative in assessing the role of selected service sectors in international trade. Specifically, we undertook the investigation of four business services—law, accounting, advertising, and management consulting.

Columbia University's location in the premier world city— where the economy is built on business services—gave Dr. Noyelle and Ms. Dutka an important comparative advantage in carrying out their inquiry. Dr. Noyelle's frequent visits to Europe in connection with research on behalf of the Organization for Economic Co-Operation and Development (OECD) also proved to be a boon for it enabled him to explore firsthand many of the factors that affect U.S. and European business service firms in that part of the world.

There is no point in summarizing the major findings that emerge from the Noyelle-Dutka inquiry. Their account is straightforward. Rather, I will offer a few observations about analytical and policy issues that remain on the agendas of both the developed and developing nations as they begin to focus on the role of services in international trade.

We know less than we need to know about the interactions between two critical dimensions of international trade in services—transborder trade and investment trade. I agree with Noyelle and Dutka that while the former will grow substantially —witness the development of software and the processing of computer data by a number of developing nations on behalf of clients from developed countries—the trend toward market segmentation and customization makes it likely that much service output in the future will need to be produced in close proximity to customers.

This observation means that where specialized human resources constitute critical inputs, developing countries must reflect upon their migration and licensing rules and regulations if they hope to benefit from those who are operating at the cutting edge. Rigidities and exclusions may retard the ability of these countries to develop a base for advanced services.

There is little reason to believe that the United States, despite its strong position as a producer of business services, can balance its international trading position simply by convincing the rest of the world to remove all or most barriers to the free movement of services. Such a policy position cannot be supported by the trade figures, by the dynamics implicit in the growth of services in less advanced economies, or by political realities. As Noyelle and Dutka point out, however, there are opportunities for reductions of barriers to trade in services that could be beneficial to all—reductions that could remain consistent with the right of independent nations to determine for themselves how far they should go in relaxing controls over critical data pools, the flow of people, licensing regulations, and other elements integral to their national sovereignty.

There will be much room for disagreement and negotiation among the GATT participants on how best to move toward reducing barriers to the international trade of services. This is not an issue that will be resolved within a year or two, or even five. In the meantime, nations must continue to expand and improve statistical bases and analytic formulations, so that policy resolutions can prove less elusive. The present effort is a useful contribution toward that goal.

—Eli Ginzberg, Director
Conservation of Human Resources
Columbia University

1

SETTING THE STAGE FOR NEGOTIATIONS ON TRADE IN SERVICES

No sooner had the United States expressed its interest in negotiating the liberalization of international trade in services in the early 1980s, than the issue became a topic of heated controversy. Clearly, that suggestion provoked widespread defensive reactions from France, Germany, India, and Brazil in telecommunications, data processing, and software; South Korea in financial services; Japan in both financial and professional services; and still other countries in other fields. Coming at a time of increasing protectionist sentiments in merchandise trade and widening U.S. trade deficits, many at first interpreted the request as an attempt by the United States to use its enormous competitive advantage in services to solve its growing trade deficit in goods at the expense of others.

Tempers have cooled somewhat since then. Heeding a call from the United States via the General Agreement on Tariffs and Trade (GATT) Council of Ministers of November 1982, several countries made special efforts to examine the issue more closely and study more carefully the implications of liberalizing trade in services. In the process, policy makers and trade negotiators around the world, including those in the United States, discovered that the underlying analytical and policy issues were often more complex than had appeared at first.

About a dozen countries, including the United States, the United Kingdom, Canada, Japan, Sweden, and the European Commission (for the European Community (EC), collectively), have now prepared and submitted to GATT their national studies on trade in services.[1] In addition, study group arrangements have been made within the United Nations Conference on Trade and Development (UNCTAD), the Organization of Economic

1

Co-Operation and Development (OECD), the Latin American Economic System (SELA), the United Nations Center on Transnational Corporations (UNCTC), and other institutions to continue to bridge the knowledge gap.[2] One result has been that a number of the countries that had first taken a highly defensive posture have come to realize that, although many services are poised to play a strategic role in future economic development, outright protectionism may not always provide the best developmental course. In addition, early expectations within the United States that a growing service trade surplus might come to compensate for the growing goods trade deficit have given place to a more realistic assessment of the limited short-term potential of such an event. In fact, there is a growing realization that a framework for liberalized trade in services will most likely take years to develop.

In short, the negotiations, as well as the learning process, have only begun. In this regard, this book is a modest contribution to the ongoing process of exploration. It is an attempt to examine key economic, historical, and institutional forces that have shaped the worldwide development of both licensed (professional) and nonlicensed business services since the end of World War II and that are likely to influence their further expansion. The objective of the analysis is to identify principal impediments and barriers to the development of international trade in business services; to point up a few of the critical conceptual issues underlying the discussion of international trade in business services; and to isolate those issues that can inform the entire service trade debate.

Throughout the book the term "international trade in business services" is used broadly to describe both direct transborder sales of services and local sales through foreign affiliates. In Chapters 6 and 7, we elaborate further on the difficulty of establishing in the service sector a clear distinction between "pure trade" (transborder sales) and "investment trade" (local sales of foreign affiliates) and on the policy implications of such findings.

The book is based on an analysis of trends in the development of the world market for four business services: legal

2

counseling, accounting, advertising, and management consulting. While legal services and accounting are subject to licensing regulations in most countries, advertising and management consulting usually are not. These four sectors were selected not only because there is considerable overlap among them, but because we were interested in investigating the extent to which nonlicensed services (such as advertising and management consulting) and licensed services (such as law and accounting) are subject to similar as well as different constraints. Two other major groups of services traditionally classified as business services, namely, computer and data processing services and architectural and engineering services are not included in our analysis.

Following this introduction, the book is organized in six chapters. Chapter 2 presents definitions and measures of business services in the United States and worldwide, including definitions and measures of the four sectors that are the focus of this study. Chapter 3 reviews the development of the world market for advertising, management consulting, accounting, and legal services, the major geographical areas of growth, and the market changes now under way. Restrictions on international trade in business services are reviewed in Chapters 4 and 5. Major impediments are presented in Chapter 4; restrictions specific to the licensed professions are discussed in Chapter 5. Chapter 6 summarizes what can be learned from the patterns of international trade in the four sectors that might inform three issues likely to be central to any negotiations on trade in services, namely:

1. The difficulty in distinguishing between pure trade and investment trade in services;

2. The importance of immigration as well as professional licensing policy issues; and,

3. Wherever applicable, the need to maintain or foster competition in both domestic and international markets for services.

Chapter 7 concludes with an examination of the trade policy implications of these analyses.

Several broad conclusions emerge from the analyses presented in this book. First, we do not believe that the processes of modernization and rationalization now underway in the production of services, which have been facilitated by advanced computerized technologies, are going to change the geography of service production to the extent that services will increasingly "behave" like goods. We recognize that computerized technology is making it increasingly possible to "can" the process of service production in the form of software and to "store" the service output in computer memories in the form of electronic digits— hence to "produce" services away from the point of consumption. Yet there are forces at least equally as powerful, both in the technology and in the evolution of markets themselves, that emphasize more than ever before the need for direct contact between firms and their clients in the course of service production. We think that this pull-push dynamic is very much in evidence not only in business services but in other service sectors as well. As a result, the notion that transborder trade is increasingly going to replace investment trade in many service sectors is, we think, misleading from both a conceptual and a policy point of view. Indeed, we believe that transborder service trade will grow mostly in complement to foreign direct investment by service firms, so that investment issues will in fact, need to receive more, not less, attention.

We also point to the need for addressing immigration policy and professional licensing policy issues. Even if transborder trade in services grows dramatically in the years ahead, for the foreseeable future it will continue to involve the movement of people—as carriers of expertise—as much as the movement of materials such as printed documents, films, videos, and electronic messages. Furthermore, since we believe that much service trade will continue to require production through local establishments, restrictions on staffing local offices will need to be addressed. Issues revolving around the granting of visas, work permits, and professional licenses will thus need special attention.

In short, we believe that developing an open trade system for a world service economy will demand the simultaneous negotiation of transborder trade, investment trade, and immigration and licensing issues—that is, the negotiation of a far more complicated set of principles than that worked out earlier to liberalize trade in goods, primarily through GATT. In particular, we suggest that some bounded notions of right of establishment and right of practice will be needed to cover those situations when trade can only be carried out through local production.

In late 1986, GATT members agreed to enter into a separate service trade negotiation within the context of a new round of multilateral negotiations. Under one proposal, an umbrella agreement would be developed that would address broad multilateral obligations required to bring about a liberalized trade regime in services in general, while sector-specific issues would be negotiated in individual sector codes or agreements. Within such a framework, sector-specific codes or agreements would emphasize issues of market access as they apply to individual sectors.

Within such a framework, as we see it, a sector-specific agreement on business services would need to address at least three such issues: improving market access of foreign business service firms to multinational clients wherever the latter need to be served; expanding access of foreign suppliers to local, domestic markets—and in particular the small- and medium-sized corporate and the public-sector procurement markets; and expanding market access of foreign firms by allowing them to diversify their offerings.

As we conclude in Chapter 7, improving market access to multinational clients and to public procurement markets are two highly desirable directions. While we also believe that liberalizing access to the small- and medium-sized corporate market is desirable, we make allowance for the fact that many countries may view this market as an appropriate area to ensure the development of native expertise and local entrepreneurship and that such objective will need to be taken into consideration during negotiations. Finally, we think that the issue of improving market access through diversification will require, as a starting point, ensuring that domestic regulations on the scope of firms' activities be applied across the board to both local and foreign firms, to avoid discriminating against foreign firms.

In conclusion, we remain struck by the extent of the knowledge gap, especially when it comes to country-specific restrictions in business service sectors and subsectors, not to mention the positive or negative impact of particular trade-restrictive policies on the development of domestic markets. We think that promoting joint study efforts in multilateral forums would be good policy in both bridging the knowledge gap and developing a shared understanding of issues and problems among the diverse parties.

Much of the information accumulated in the course of our research was developed through extensive interviews with government officials, policy makers, and senior managers of business service firms in both the United States and several West European countries. We have respected the wishes of many of our interviewees and avoided explicit reference to individual firms, except for information available in the public domain. Unless otherwise referenced, factual information presented in this study is based on these interviews. We remain most grateful to the many individuals who lent us time, patience, and assistance throughout the course of this study. In particular, we wish to thank John Alic, Michael Balfour, Etienne Barbier, Claude Barfield, Axel Baum, Roger Berg, Alain Bouldouyre, Peter Daniels, François Ecalle, Peter Edwards, Raymond Eeckhout, André Faures, Geza Feketekuty, Laurent Gaillot, Jeffrey Hart, Charles Heeter, Jack Hutchings, John Jackson, Thomas B. Kelly, Ed Kiernan, Michael Krieff, Stuart Marx, Michael Maunsell, Frank Monhart, Richard Nerard, Walter O'Connor, Gardner Patterson, Jean Raffegeau, John B. Richardson, Richard Selp, Jerome G. Shapiro, Steve Solario, Jean-François Tessler, the other participants in the AEI Trade in Services project, and our colleagues Thomas Bailey, Eli Ginzberg, and Thomas Stanback at Conservation of Human Resources.

In the final analysis, however, the interpretation of the evidence presented in this book is ours and ours only.

NOTES

1. See, for example, Office of the U.S. Trade Representative, *U.S. National Study on Trade in Services* (Washington, December 1983), and European Communities, *Study on International Trade in Services*, Document I-420-84-EN (Brussels, 1984).
2. Karl Sauvant, *International Trade in Services: The Politics of Transborder Data Flows* (Boulder, Colo.: Westview Press, 1987).

2

BUSINESS SERVICES
Measurements and Definitions

Aside from periodic reporting by the business press on individual law firms, advertising agencies, consulting houses, or accounting firms, business services remain poorly understood by most economists, policy makers, and others who might need to be better informed about them. This is the case in part because, until their explosive growth in the 1980s, business services were regarded, wrongly or rightfully, as arcane areas of economic activities that had grown mostly as a result of demand from a selected group of large corporate customers and were not particularly significant for the broader economy. The fact that these sectors had traditionally received little attention from government statisticians further clouded perceptions regarding their economic importance.

This chapter reviews what is known from official sources about those industries. In addition, it looks at definitional and measurement problems stemming from the earlier lack of statistical precision, as well as from the fluidity of sector boundaries in periods of rapid development.

MEASURING BUSINESS SERVICES

The U.S. Market

In 1984, the most recent year for which detailed data are available, U.S. output in business services amounted to nearly $250 billion—approximately 6.8 percent of the U.S. gross national product (GNP). This represented a sharp rise from 1977, when the sector's output stood at $90 billion, or 4.7 percent of the GNP (see Table 2–1). In 1982, the latest year for which detailed data are available, business service industries employed approximately 4.7 million persons, or slightly over 5 percent of the nation's total nonagricultural employment, compared to a 6.4 percent share of the GNP. Such difference between employment and GNP shares reflected, in part, the high–value added nature of such activities.

Broadly defined, and in keeping with the U.S. Standard Industrial Code (SIC), business service industries include: the business services group (SIC 73), with large components such as advertising (SIC 731), computer and data processing (SIC 737), and management, consulting, and public relations services (SIC 7392); the legal services group (SIC 81); and the miscellaneous services group (SIC 89), with such major sub-components as engineering, architectural, and surveying services (SIC 891), and accounting, auditing, and bookkeeping services (SIC 893). Compound annual rates of growth over the periods 1972–1977 and 1977–1984, shown in the last two columns of Table 2–1, point to the phenomenal expansion of these services during those years. Between 1977 and 1984 in particular, compound annual rates of growth in such sectors as advertising, computer and data processing, and management, consulting, and public relations services rose to be approximately twice as large as the corresponding rate for the gross national product. In the other sectors, rates of growth were at least 60 percent higher than for the GNP.

Clearly, the very growth of these sectors wreaked havoc with a statistical national accounting system originally designed to record changes in manufacturing or other traditional service sectors, such as trade and finance, not changes in the relatively newer business services. This problem is well known and needs no extensive discussion.[1] The following examples emphasize the limitations faced in trying to assess changes in sectors for which measures are so poor:

- Prior to the *1977 Census of Services*, the Bureau of the Census did not survey the accounting, auditing, and bookkeeping industries!

Table 2–1. Business Services in the United States: Gross Receipts of Establishments with Payroll, 1972 to 1984 ($ billions).

Sectors and Subsectors (by SIC Code)	1972	1977	1982	1984 (Estimate)	Compound Annual Rates of Growth	
					1972–77	1977–84
73 Business services (subtotal)	35.5	50.0	111.4	148.3	7.1	16.8
731 Advertising	2.3	4.5	8.4	13.8	14.4	17.4
7311 Advertising agencies	1.8	3.2	5.9	9.9	12.1	17.2
737 Computer and data processing	3.4	7.5	22.7	26.1	17.2	19.4
739 Other business services (subtotal)						
7392 Management, consulting, and public relations	3.6	6.7	18.0	27.8	13.2	22.5
pt 1 Management and administrative services	3.3[a]	6.2[a]	4.2	n.a.	n.a.	n.a.
pt 2 Management consulting			6.0	n.a.	n.a.	n.a.
pt 3 Economic research			2.6	n.a.	n.a.	n.a.
pt 4 Consulting services			2.1	n.a.	n.a.	n.a.
pt 5 Public relations	0.3	0.5	1.1	n.a.	n.a.	n.a.
81 Legal services (subtotal)	9.7	17.4	34.7	44.9	12.3	14.5
811 pt 1 Legal services	9.7	17.1	34.3	n.a.	n.a.	n.a.
811 pt 2 Legal aid societies, etc.	n.a.	0.3	0.4	n.a.	n.a.	n.a.
89 Miscellaneous services (subtotal)	n.a.	21.4	48.1	55.9	n.a.	14.7
891 Engineering, architectural, and surveying	7.6	14.1	33.5	36.6	13.2	14.6
893 Accounting, auditing, and bookkeeping	n.a.	7.3	14.6	19.3	n.a.	14.9
Total SIC 73, 81, 89	n.a.	89.3	194.2	249.1	n.a.	15.8
Gross national product	1,185.9	1,918.3	3,069.3	3,662.8	10.1	9.6

Source: U.S. Bureau of the Census, *Census of Services,* for 1972, 1977, and 1982. Estimates for 1984 are from U.S. Bureau of the Census, *Current Business Reports, Series BS, 1984 Service Annual Survey.*

a. Combined gross receipts for parts 1, 2, 3, and 4 (SIC 7392).

- Prior to 1967, the computer and data processing services group—which today includes not only data processing bureaus but also on-line data base services and software houses—was combined with the management consulting services group.

- Prior to the *1982 Census of Services*, the management, consulting, and public relations group was disaggregated into only two subgroups: management and consulting services, and public relations services. The management and consulting services group was then a hodgepodge of services ranging from administrative services rendered to motels through franchising contracts to economic research or management consulting. Since the 1982 census, this group has been disaggregated into four major subgroups (see Table 2–1).

The World Market

Official estimates of the magnitude of the world market for business services do not exist. Based on limited available data on the market shares of the largest firms both in the United States and worldwide, we estimate that the world market for advertising agencies, management consulting firms, and accounting firms was approximately twice the size of the U.S. market in 1984: $20 billion, $20 billion, and $40 billion, respectively (see Table 2–2).[2] For legal services, we found no reliable way to develop a reasonable estimate of the size of the world market.

International Trade

Accurate measurements of international trade in business services are also difficult to come by. The 1983 *U.S. National Study on Trade in Services* (the U.S. government's response to GATT's 1982 request for individual country studies on trade in the services) gives estimates of world service exports (nonfactor

Table 2–2. World Receipts in Four Business Services, 1984 ($ billions).

Service Type	World Market (Estimate)	U.S. Market
Advertising agencies	20.0	9.9
Management consulting	20.0	9.3
Accounting	40.0	19.3
Legal services	n.a.	44.5

Source: See U.S. Bureau of the Census, *Current Business Reports, Series BS, 1984 Service Annual Survey* for U.S. market measures. See ch. 2, n. 2 for sources for world market estimates.

income) for 1980 amounting to nearly $370 billion, or about 20 percent of world trade.[3] These are based on balance of payments data collected worldwide by the Bank for International Settlements (BIS) in Basel and prepared, in the United States, by the Bureau of Economic Analysis (BEA) of the Department of Commerce. (Matching data for goods trade in the same year indicate a much higher global export value of goods—nearly $1,650 billion.) According to the same BIS series, the United States was the leading exporter of services in 1980 with $37.5 billion worth of exports, followed closely by the United Kingdom ($37.1 billion), West Germany ($33.8 billion), and France ($33 billion). Italy ranked fifth ($23.5 billion), and Japan sixth ($19.4 billion) (see Table 2–3).

What is the contribution of business services to U.S. service exports? BEA's most recent balance of payments data suggest that total service exports (excluding investment income) amounted to $46 billion in 1985 ($35.3 billion in 1980), including $29 billion in transportation and transportation-related services, $8.5 billion worth of exports in "other private services," and $8.5 billion in fees and royalties (see Table 2–4).

However, such data have come under considerable criticism for seriously underestimating service trade not directly related to transportation and travel. Most recently, these figures have been reexamined by the Office of Technology Assessment (OTA), the

Table 2–3. Leading Exporters of Services, 1980 ($ billions).

United States	37.5
United Kingdom	37.1
West Germany	33.8
France	33.0
Italy	23.5
Japan	19.4
Netherlands	18.6
Belgium	14.9
Spain	12.2
Austria	10.8
Subtotal	240.8
World Exports	370.0

Source: Office of the U.S. Trade Representative, *U.S. National Study on Trade in Services* (Washington, 1983), Appendix I, Table 2, p. 112.

congressional research arm, as part of a broad assessment of U.S. competitiveness in service industries.[4]

To assess the impact of service trade on the U.S. economy, OTA used two concepts:

- *U.S. exports* (based on a balance of payments concept): this measure includes export sales of all firms located in the United States, including sales to overseas affiliates of U.S. firms and the exports of U.S.-based, foreign-owned firms;

- *Foreign revenues of U.S. firms* (based on an ownership concept): this measure includes foreign sales of all U.S.-owned firms regardless of location, including both exports from the United States of U.S.-owned firms and sales to foreign entities by overseas U.S. firms. Transactions between U.S. parent and foreign affiliates are excluded as both buyer and seller are U.S.-owned; transactions between U.S.-owned firms located overseas and unaffiliated U.S. firms are excluded for the same reason.[5]

Table 2–4. Service Exports and Investment Income in U.S. Balance of Payments, 1980 and 1985 ($ billions).

	1980	1985 (Estimate)
All services (nonfactor income)	35.3	46.0
Travel	10.0	11.7
Passenger fares	2.6	3.0
Other transportation	11.0	14.3
Fees and royalties	7.0	8.5
Other private services	4.7	8.5
Income on Investment (factor income)	56.7	89.6
All services and investment income (invisible receipts)	92.0	135.6

Source: U.S. Department of Commerce, Bureau of Economic Analysis, *Survey of Current Business* (June 1981 and March 1986).

OTA used a parallel set of definitions to develop estimates on the import side. Strictly speaking, a complete picture of trade in services on an ownership basis should also have included purchases of services in the United States by foreign-owned firms located in the United States and local purchases by U.S.-owned firms abroad. The lack of appropriate data made such estimations impossible. In 1982, however, nonbank U.S. affiliates of nonbank foreign firms made purchases of $440 billion after taxes, exclusive of employee compensation and nonoperating expenses. Some undefined portion of these purchases represented local purchases of services used in the course of operations.[6]

Table 2–5 summarizes OTA's mid-range estimates of exports and imports for 1983; Table 2–6 shows OTA's mid-range estimates of foreign revenues of U.S. firms and U.S. revenues of foreign firms for the same year.

OTA's mid-range export and import estimates for 1983 are considerably higher than those of BEA. OTA estimates service exports at $76 billion in 1983, a measure nearly twice as large as BEA's estimate of $41.8 billion. Likewise, OTA's import measure

Table 2–5. OTA Mid-range Estimates of Service Balance of Payments, 1983 ($ billions).

Service Type	Exports (Receipts)	Imports (Payments)
Accounting	0.35	a
Advertising	0.30	a
Construction	4.80	0.85
Data processing	0.65	1.00
Education	1.95	0.20
Engineering	1.35	0.20
Franchising	0.65	a
Health	1.75	a
Information	1.45	0.50
Insurance	7.15	7.90
Investment banking/brokerage	4.80	4.55
Leasing	0.70	0.50
Legal	1.00	0.50
Licensing	5.20	0.80
Management/consulting	1.00	0.85
Motion pictures	1.90	0.90
Retailing	a	a
Software	2.55	1.10
Telecommunications	1.30	2.20
Transportation	17.10	19.10
Travel	14.10	15.80
Miscellaneous	5.30	1.90
OTA mid-range estimate	75.4	58.9
BEA total	41.8	35.4

Source: U.S. Congress, Office of Technology Assessment, *Trade in Services: Exports and Foreign Revenues*, Special Report OTA-ITA-316 (Washington, September 1986), p. 38.

a. Negligible.

runs at $59 billion in 1983, compared to $35.4 billion for BEA (see Table 2–5).

Foreign revenues of U.S. service firms are estimated at $160.5 billion in 1983 by OTA, including $92.4 billion worth of sales through foreign-based affiliates and $68.1 billion worth of direct exports. For the same year, OTA estimates U.S. revenues of foreign service firms to have stood at $122 billion, including

Table 2–6. OTA Estimates of Foreign Revenues of U.S. Service Firms and U.S. Revenue of Foreign Service Firms, 1983 ($ billions).

Service Type	Foreign Revenues of U.S. Service Firms			U.S. Revenues of Foreign Service Firms		
	Direct Exports	Affiliate Sales	Total Foreign Revenues	Direct Imports	Affiliate Sales	Total Foreign Revenues
Accounting	0.35	3.85	4.20	a	0.80	0.80
Advertising	0.40	1.70	2.00	a	0.20	0.20
Construction	4.80	3.10	7.90	1.35	3.20	4.05
Data processing	0.65	3.10	3.75	1.00	0.10	1.10
Education	1.95	0.05	2.00	0.20	a	0.20
Engineering	1.35	4.00	5.30	0.20	0.90	1.10
Franchising	0.65	a	0.65	a	a	a
Health	1.75	1.10	2.85	a	0.40	0.40
Information	1.45	1.45	2.90	0.50	0.50	1.00
Insurance	3.35	11.10	16.75	4.50	15.60	20.10
Investment banking/brokerage	1.50	7.70	9.20	0.25	7.80	8.05
Leasing	0.60	4.55	5.05	0.50	0.25	0.75
Legal	1.00	0.10	1.10	0.50	a	0.50
Licensing	5.20	a	5.20	0.80	a	0.40
Management/consulting	1.00	1.20	2.20	0.25	0.10	0.35
Motion pictures	1.90	2.00	3.90	0.90	1.00	1.90
Retailing	a	25.40	25.40	a	32.10	32.10
Software	2.55	3.80	6.35	1.10	0.10	1.20
Telecommunications	1.30	1.30	2.60	2.00	0.30	2.30
Transportation	17.10	10.90	28.00	19.10	5.10	24.20
Travel	14.10	a	14.10	15.80	a	15.80
Miscellaneous	5.30	6.00	11.30	1.90	3.20	5.10
Total	68.10	92.40	160.50	50.35	71.60	122.00

Source: U.S. Congress, Office of Technology Assessment, *Trade in Services: Exports and Foreign Revenues*, Special Report OTA-ITE-316 (Washington, September 1986), pp. 41 and 42.

a. Negligible.

$71.6 billion worth of affiliate sales and $50.3 billion worth of direct imports (see Table 2–6).

Note that for conceptual reasons explained in its report, OTA excludes exports and foreign revenues of several service sectors, including commercial banking and wholesaling, from these estimates.[7]

Table 2–7 summarizes OTA's detailed estimates for the four sectors that are the subjects of our analysis for 1982, 1983, and 1984. OTA's measure suggests the following:

1. Foreign revenues of the U.S. advertising and accounting firms are generated mostly through affiliate sales. OTA estimates such revenues at approximately $2 billion and $4.2 billion, respectively, for 1983.

2. Foreign revenues of U.S. consulting firms are generated somewhat more evenly through direct export and affiliate sales. OTA estimates such revenues at approximately $2.2 billion for 1983.

3. In advertising, accounting, and management consulting, foreign revenues of U.S. service firms may account for nearly one-fourth of the market outside the United States (compare Tables 2–2 and 2–7).

4. Only in legal services does the importance of foreign revenues of U.S. firms relative to domestic revenues seem small (compare Tables 2–2 and 2–7). OTA estimates such revenues at approximately $1 billion for 1983. It may be useful to point out that foreign revenues of U.S. law firms are likely to be generated mostly in the form of domestic sales of services to U.S. affiliates of foreign firms—that is, in the very form that OTA was unable to estimate. (See Chapter 3 for a discussion of the firm-client relationship in the legal services industry.)

Looking at the four sectors together, the patterns of trade identified by OTA—especially the split between pure trade and

Table 2–7.   OTA Estimates of Foreign Revenues of U.S. Service Firms and U.S. Revenues of Foreign Firms in Four Business Services, 1982, 1983, and 1984 ($ billions).

Service Type	1982	1983	1984
Advertising			
Foreign revenues of U.S. firms			
Direct exports	0.1–0.5	0.1–0.5	0.1–0.5
Affiliate sales	1.6	1.7	1.8
Majority-owned	1.4	1.5	n.a.
Minority-owned	0.2	0.2	n.a.
Subtotal	1.7–2.1	1.8–2.2	1.9–2.3
U.S. revenues of foreign firms			
Direct imports	a	a	a
Affiliate sales	0.2	0.2	n.a.
Joint ventures	n.a.	n.a.	n.a.
Management consulting			
Foreign revenues of U.S. firms			
Direct exports	0.5–1.1	0.6–1.4	0.6–1.6
Affiliate sales	1.2	1.2	n.a.
Majority-owned	1.2	1.2	n.a.
Minority-owned	a	a	n.a.
Subtotal	1.7–2.3	1.8–2.6	n.a.
U.S. revenues of foreign firms			
Direct imports	0.0–0.5	0.0–0.5	0.0–0.5
Affiliate sales	n.a.	0.1	n.a.
Subtotal	n.a.	0.1–0.6	n.a.
Accounting			
Foreign revenues of U.S. firms			
Direct exports	0.2–0.5	0.2–0.5	0.2–0.5
Affiliate sales	3.6–3.9	3.7–4.0	3.9–4.2
Subtotal	3.8–4.4	3.9–4.5	4.1–4.7
U.S. revenues of foreign firms			
Direct imports	a	a	a
Affiliate sales	0.6–0.8	0.7–0.9	0.8–1.0
Legal services			
Foreign revenues of U.S. firms			
Direct exports	0.0–2.0	0.0–2.0	0.0–2.0
Affiliate sales	0.1	0.1	n.a.
Subtotal	0.1–2.1	0.1–2.1	n.a.
U.S. revenues of foreign firms			
Direct imports	0.0–1.0	0.0–1.0	0.0–1.0
Affiliate sales	a	a	a
Subtotal	0.0–1.0	0.0–1.0	0.0–1.0

Source: U.S. Congress, Office of Technology Assessment, *Trade in Services: Exports and Foreign Revenues*, Special Report OTA-ITE-316 (Washington, September 1986), pp. 50, 52, 83, and 87.

a. Negligible

19

investment trade—appear highly consistent with our own interview-based assessment presented in the next chapters.

DEFINING BUSINESS SERVICES

Today even BEA is ready to concede that OTA's most recent estimations are better than its own. Great caution must still be exercised, however, when using many of these service trade data. In its own report, OTA makes a number of recommendations for improving surveys of service trade.[8] But improvements in the measurements are likely to be difficult to achieve, not only because of the time and resources needed to implement recommended improvements, but also because weaknesses in trade measures are linked to weaknesses in the measurement of domestic output. In turn, these measurement weaknesses derive from problems of sector definitions.

One major difficulty stems from the fact that many of the business service sectors are either too new or too fast-changing, or both, to have well-established market boundaries. A number of the sectors have developed as an outgrowth of others and lack a solid measurement base. Undermeasurement remains rampant in the business service sector, be it in trade terms or in domestic output terms.

To return to a couple of the examples mentioned earlier, data processing bureaus in the old days of electromechanical data processing were few in number and had developed as an extension of the management consulting industry. The introduction of electronic data processing and the rapid growth in demand for such services in the 1960s resulted in sufficient market differentiation to bring about the emergence of firms specializing in just this area of activities. Automated Data Processing (ADP) in New Jersey and Electronic Data Services (EDS) in Texas—recently sold to General Motors—are only two of the most successful bureaus to have emerged as a result of the explosive growth of electronic data processing at that time. Later, even further differentiation emerged among data processing bureaus, on-line data base services, and software houses. A number of today's largest software houses started out as management consulting firms back in the 1960s and developed their software business working on large computer systems contracts for federal agencies and the military.

Management consulting itself underwent a process of differentiation not unlike that experienced by the data processing industry. Today a number of fairly distinct industries are identified under the management, consulting, and public relations grouping, including public relations, economic research (Chase Econometrics, Wharton Forecasting), management contract services (Quality Inn, Motel 6), and traditional management consulting. In its present configuration, management consulting can best be defined as an area of services offering expertise in the development of managerial systems, ranging from management information and personnel systems (compensation plans, pension plans, actuarial work) to office, manufacturing, production, marketing, and distribution systems.[9]

A second source of difficulty stems from considerable overlap among different business services. In the United States, for example, a number of advertising firms are extensively involved in public relations work, market opinion survey work, or other lines of work similar to those handled by management consulting firms.[10] Likewise, large U.S. law firms, traditionally focused on business law (for example, antitrust, international business law, financial law), are doing an increasing amount of work in areas of tax, trust, and estates, as are some accounting firms. Today between 20 and 40 percent of the gross receipts of the largest accounting firms are from tax work and management advisory services (MAS), the latter being simply another term for what is more commonly known as management consulting (see Chapters 3 and 6).[11]

Another complexity arises from the difficulties in comparing country-specific institutional and professional arrangements. The accounting, advertising, management consulting, and legal sectors may give rise to very different business organizations, depending on the country of origin, but all these organizations nevertheless compete in the same world markets. This is no small matter since any meaningful attempt at liberalizing trade requires at some point normalization of the scope of business within given geographical markets among organizations from different points of origin.

Perhaps the most complex situation in this respect is that found in legal services. While we return to this example several times in this book, it may be helpful to take a brief look at it early on.

In the United States, lawyers are organized in a single profession, and legal professionals are typically members of a state bar. U.S. business lawyers, who are of most direct concern to us in this study, are employed either as legal counsels by corporations or as associates and partners by law firms, whose services are hired by clients.

In the United Kingdom, business lawyers are typically "solicitors," to be distinguished from "barristers." Barristers have a monopoly over court work and as a result tend to control a great deal of the litigation work. Solicitors, by comparison, will tend to handle business and international law, tax, and trust work.

Throughout most of continental Europe, where the Napoleonic legal system prevails, the legal professions are split even further, typically into three professions: *avocats, notaires*, and *counseils juridiques*. France used to distinguish further between *avocats* and *avoués*, but the distinction was eliminated in the mid-1960s.

Under the French system, for example, *avocats* have a monopoly over court work, are appointed to a bar, and handle most litigation work. In a sense, they approximate the English barrister. *Notaires* have a monopoly over the recorded instruments and documents that are critical to a legal system in which codified rules dominate over court-litigated decisions. They control much of the trust business, do tax work, broker real estate, manage assets for individuals or corporations, and handle financial placements. In the United States, such transactions would have to be handled, respectively, by real estate brokers, investment bankers, or fund managers. Lastly, the *conseil juridique*, which has evolved at the periphery of the other two legal professions, comes closest to the American role of a business lawyer. This type of practitioner focuses on international law, business law, and tax work. His or her access to the domestic court system is extremely restricted. U.S. law firms operating in France operate under a *conseil juridique* status. Still, because tax work may represent a large share of their revenues, *conseils juridiques* can often compete directly with accounting firms.

For example, Bureau Francis LeFebvre, Conseils Juridiques et Fiscaux, probably the largest *conseil juridique* in France, is a firm that specializes in business law and tax work and employs over 300 people (half professionals and half support staff). One-half of the firm's fees are generated through tax work and the other half through legal work. While the firm is known throughout Europe for its expertise on North Africa, the Middle East, and French-speaking Africa, and for dealing mostly with blue chip corporate clients, its product mix is not unusual in France. Many of the *fiduciaires*—the large French accounting firms specializing in straight bookkeeping and accounting work, to be distinguished from the *cabinets de revision comptable* that specialize in audits and are closer to the Anglo-American auditing firm (see Chapter 5)—have traditionally owned *conseils juridiques et fiscaux* subsidiaries.

CONCLUSIONS

Business services, including the four sectors under study in this book, have experienced both rapid growth and extensive transformation over the past ten years or so. Partly as a result, measurement of many of these sectors—be it in terms of domestic output or of trade—is plagued by serious limitations. At the same time, however, this rapid growth is in no small way a reflection of the growing strategic importance of business services. This is why, of course, business services have the potential to become one of the major stakes in future trade discussions, regardless of our ability to define or measure these sectors.

OTA's recent assessment of U.S. trade in services suggests that, in accounting and advertising, foreign revenues are generated principally through investment trade (that is, through foreign affiliates), whereas management consulting revenues originate both through direct trade and investment trade. In all three sectors foreign revenues appear to constitute a large share of the revenues of U.S. firms. By comparison, in law, foreign revenues of U.S. firms appear small relative to total domestic revenues of the industry. This is most likely because a good deal of the foreign revenues of the industry are generated through transactions not traditionally counted in trade measures, be they conventional balance of payments measures or even OTA's expanded foreign revenues measures.

NOTES

1. See, for example, Ronald K. Shelp, "Growing Trade," *Policy Options* 7, no. 8 (October 1986) published by the Institute for Research on Public Policy, (Halifax South, Nova Scotia).
2. These are crude estimates based on indirect evidence of market share of U.S. firms in foreign markets as presented in *Advertising Age* (various issues); *International Accounting Bulletin* (various issues); Thierry J. Noyelle, *The Coming of Age of Management Consulting: Implications for New York City*, Report to New York City's Office of Economic Development, 1984; and U.S. Congress Office of Technology Assessment, *Trade in Services: Exports and Foreign Revenues*, Special Report, Washington: U.S. Government Printing Office, OTA-ITE-316, September 1986.
3. *U.S. National Study on Trade in Services*, Appendix I, p. 11.
4. OTA, *Trade in Services*.
5. Ibid., p. 17.
6. Ibid., p. 17.
7. Ibid., pp. 53–58.
8. Ibid., pp. 5–11.
9. Some of these examples are taken from Noyelle, *The Coming of Age of Management Consulting*.
10. Ibid.
11. *International Accounting Bulletin* (December 1984).

3

THE DEVELOPMENT OF A WORLD MARKET FOR BUSINESS SERVICES

While most business services have changed considerably over the recent past, and while some do represent rather new activities, many find their roots in earlier times. In the United Kingdom, France, and the United States, advertising emerged at the end of the nineteenth century, experiencing its first major phase of growth during the 1910s and 1920s. The seeds of a modern accounting industry were planted in the United Kingdom during the nineteenth century. Legally mandated, certified audits were introduced in the United States early in this century, giving impetus to the growth of the accounting industry in that country.[1] Likewise, management consulting traces its roots to the "industrial engineering" and "time and motion studies" pioneered by Frederick W. Taylor, Frank and Lillian Gilbreth, Harrington Emerson, and others at the turn of the century.[2]

Nevertheless, the early post–World War II years marked a major turning point in the role played by business services.[3] During those years, business services grew from being mostly peripheral industries to become increasingly critical components in the workings of business and the economy at large. Along with other sectors such as telecommunications and banking, and not unlike transportation and commerce somewhat earlier, business services began to acquire a new importance, placing them increasingly at the center of a structural transformation referred to alternately as the advent of the "service economy" or the rise of the "postindustrial economy."

It is because the advent of the service economy may represent as fundamental a transformation as the transition from an agricultural to an industrial economy that the analysis of the development of the world market for business services must be placed within a broad economic and institutional context. Otherwise, we shall miss the proper frame of reference for identifying the factors that are relevant to the future development of this market. More broadly, we might fail to recognize that problems of trade in professional business services, rather than being exceptional, are in fact indicative of a wide range of issues originating in the advent of a service economy characterized by extensive worldwide integration of markets.

THE DEVELOPMENT OF THE U.S.
MARKET FOR BUSINESS SERVICES

As Stanback et al. have pointed out in *Services/The New Economy*, the rise of services in the United States economy underscores the dual transformation in *what* the economy produces and, most importantly, in *how* it produces.[4] In terms of final outputs—that is, of *what* is being produced—the post–World War II decades have been marked by increasing consumption of services—at first, mostly public-sector services; later, increasingly educational and medical services. In part, this shift simply reflects growing wealth and rising discretionary spending for services that in earlier times might not have been considered necessities of life.

More importantly, perhaps, the advent of the service economy also represents a fundamental transformation in *how* the economy produces final outputs—both goods and services—and is marked by the formidable growth of "intermediate service inputs," which are purchased by firms at intermediate stages of production.

An example of the transformation under way can be found in automobile manufacturing. Instead of continuing to employ large numbers of blue-collar workers on assembly lines or in the shops of parts suppliers, manufacturers are now replacing workers with robots. In turn this development is leading to an increasing demand for engineers to design and develop new products, systems analysts and programmers to develop the

Table 3–1.   Shares of Full-Time Equivalent Employment and Gross National Product by Industry, 1947 and 1982.

| | 1947 | | 1982 | |
Industry Type	Empl.	GNP[a]	Empl.	GNP[a]
Nonservice industries (subtotal)	43.4	37.4	28.7	30.2
Agriculture, mining, construction	11.1	12.9	7.2	7.6
Manufacturing	32.3	24.5	21.5	22.6
Service industries (subtotal)	56.6	62.6	71.3	69.8
Transportation communication, wholesaling	13.5	13.4	11.7	16.5
Financial services and business services	6.1	15.5	13.9	23.7
Retail and other consumer services	20.2	16.5	19.2	12.2
Nonprofit education and health	2.6	2.7	7.5	5.3
Public sector and public education	14.2	14.6	19.1	12.0
All industries	100.0	100.0	100.0	100.0

Source: U.S. Department of Commerce, Bureau of Economic Analysis, *National Income and Product Accounts of the U.S. 1929–1974* and *Survey of Current Business*, July 1983, Tables 6.2B and 6.8B. Updated from Thomas M.Stanback, Peter J. Bearse, Thierry J. Noyelle, and Robert A. Karasek, *Services/The New Economy* (Totowa, N.J.: Rowman and Allanheld, 1981).

a. GNP shares are computed on the basis of constant 1972 dollars.

softwares needed to run CAD/CAM technologies, and technicians and other skilled workers to program and manage the robots on the shop floors. In short, the shift toward services does not mean that the economy is no longer producing goods, but simply that goods are being produced in a much different way than they were during the earlier industrial period. The result is an increasing demand for white-collar personnel and for intermediate service inputs ranging from transportation, communications, and wholesaling to banking, financial, and business services.

The rising importance of intermediate services in the U.S. economy is shown in Table 3–1. Between 1947 and 1982, the employment share of transportation, communication, wholesaling, financial services, and business services rose from less than 20 percent to slightly over 25 percent. Far more impressive was the concomitant change in the share of GNP originating in those same sectors, which grew from less than 29 percent in 1947 to nearly 40 percent in 1982!

Two forces in particular contributed to the expansion of business services. First, demand for such services grew as they became an increasingly integral part of the new ways of doing business. For example, the expanded use of auditing services resulted in better accounting control systems and, in turn, better controls over costs and productivity. Likewise, better opinion survey work resulted in more accurate knowledge of consumer demand and, ultimately, expanded opportunities for larger profits by firms.

Secondly, the growth of business services was propelled by the increasing externalization of service functions by user firms. Services traditionally produced in-house were increasingly contracted out. For instance, while firms might once have kept track of tax changes for themselves, the market became large enough that user firms could turn to large law or accounting firms to purchase tax expertise. In addition, such contracted expertise was likely to be better and ultimately cheaper than in-house expertise.

At first much of the demand for business services originated in the largest industrial corporations, which is why the internationalization of American business service firms closely followed the foreign expansion of their industrial clients. This may be changing, however. In the most advanced economies, including those of the United States and Western Europe, there is a burgeoning demand for business services from the middle- and small-sized corporate market and even from individuals. Such demand tends to be highly atomistic and necessitates a fundamental shift in market strategy on the part of business service firms if they are to capture the potential revenues and profits associated with these relatively newer markets. Typically, this requires shifting from a follow-the-leader to a become-the-leader strategy. Rather than having the demand of large corporations structure the supply of business service firms, the latter must now structure the demand for their services. Indeed, there is evidence of a shift whereby regional, national, or multinational expansion is increasingly guided by the business service firm's assessment of the potential of these new, mostly local markets, less by the demand of the large national or multinational corporations.[5] This is not unlike what happened earlier in corporate middle-market banking and in retail banking. Since those smaller markets may well become tomorrow's greatest growth and profit opportunities, it may be there that countries will become most concerned with ensuring the development of a base of local service firms. We return to this issue in Chapter 6.

This being said, the fact remains that, historically, the industrial multinationals paved the way for the business service multinationals. As they moved abroad, first to Western Europe and later to other regions of the world, U.S. business service firms often found that local firms had limited business expertise to offer. As a result, U.S. firms played a key role in many countries in "creating" a domestic market. U.S. advertising agencies, for example, consider that for all practical purposes they created the advertising industry and opened up the principal markets both here and abroad (the first half of this assertion is likely to be hotly contested by the French, who will point to Havas Conseil as the first advertising agency ever opened). Today's accounting industry is also largely an American creation, although in fairness to British accounting firms, they were the first to internationalize. After World War II, however, most of the largest U.K. firms were merged with U.S. firms, which quickly proceeded to take the lead.[6] Similarly, in what is commonly called "international business law," U.S. law firms broke much new ground, especially in financial legal areas, although British solicitors and the Commonwealth courts originally played a key role in developing maritime law.

THE INTERNATIONALIZATION OF U.S. FIRMS AND THE CREATION OF A WORLD MARKET FOR BUSINESS SERVICES

The internationalization of U.S. professional business service firms between the early 1960s and the mid-1980s is shown in

Table 3–2. Arthur Andersen's Offices outside the United States, 1960, 1974, and 1983.

	Number of Offices		
	1960	1974	1983
Canada	1	5	7
Western Europe	6	21	50
Latin America and Caribbean	12	13	19
Asia and Pacific Area	0	8	17[a]
Africa and the Middle East	0	1	12[b]

Source: Arthur Andersen & Co., *The First Sixty Years: 1913–1973* (Chicago: Arthur Andersen & Co., 1974), pp. 53–54. Also from Arthur Andersen & Co. office directories, various years.

a. Includes a collaboration agreement with six local firms in six countries.

b. Includes a collaboration agreement with one firm in one country.

Tables 3–2, 3–3, and 3–4 for accounting, Tables 3–5 and 3–6 for advertising, Tables 3–7 and 3–8 for management consulting, and Tables 3–9 and 3–10 for legal services. While these tables reveal the strong influence of the economics of the firm-client relationship on the pattern of internationalization by U.S. business service firms, the impact of national regulatory barriers and restrictions cannot be ignored. In the following paragraphs, we pay particular attention to the economics of the firm-client relationship; in the next two chapters, we will review in more detail the influence of regulations and restrictions.

Accounting

Table 3–2 shows the pattern of expansion of Arthur Andersen outside the United States between 1960 and 1983. During that period, the firm's foreign offices grew in number from 19 to 105. In a pattern similar to that found among its principal competitors, Arthur Andersen's expansion focused at first on Western Europe and Latin America, later on Asia and the Pacific region, Africa, and the Middle East.[7]

Table 3–3. Worldwide Offices of the Thirteen Largest Accounting Firms, 1982 (ranked by worldwide sales).

World Rank	Firm	North America	Europe	Latin America and Caribbean	Asia and Pacific Area	Africa and Middle East	Worldwide Total
1	Arthur Andersen	83	42	20	11	10	166
2	Peat Marwick Intl	122	76	42	69	42	351
3	Coopers and Lybrand Intl	108	137	36	97	52	430
4	Price Waterhouse	107	74	59	68	43	351
5	Klynveld Main Goerdder	129	153	25	52	35	394
6	Ernst & Whinney Intl	131	66	41	58	36	332
7	Arthur Young Intl	92	89	18	34	18	251
8	Deloitte Haskins & Sells	139	148	30	82	46	445
9	Touche Ross Intl	107	130	37	80	45	399
10	Binder Dijker Otte	101	105	5	13	14	238
11	Grant Thornton Intl	107	112	39	27	20	305
12	Howarth & Howarth Intl	44	54	16	25	12	151
13	Fox Moore Intl	62	37	2	15	9	125

Source: Vinod B. Bavishi and Harold E. Wyman, *Who Audits the World: Trends in the Worldwide Accounting Profession* (Storrs, CT: University of Connecticut Center for Transnational Accounting and Financial Research, 1983). pp. 36, 37, 39.

Table 3–4. Worldwide Fees of the Fifteen Largest Accounting Firms, 1983 ($ millions).

World Rank	International Affiliation	Worldwide Fees	U.S. Fees	Non-U.S. Fees	Percentage of Distribution of Worldwide Fees By Type			All Staff
					Audit	Tax	MAS[a]	
1	Arthur Andersen	1,238	909	329	52	21	27	24,292
2	Peat Marwick Intl	1,230	750	480	77	15	8	27,000
3	Coopers & Lybrand Intl	1,100	625	475	70	15	15	30,000[b]
4	Price Waterhouse	1,100	493	610	69	20	11	25,141
5	Klynveld Main Goerdder	1,000	179	821	76	12	12	29,500
6	Ernst & Whinney Intl	972	625	347	69	17	14	21,500
7	Arthur Young Intl	955	440	515		n.a.		23,040
8	Deloitte Haskins & Sells	900	415	485	74	11	15	25,760
9	Touche Ross Intl	900[b]	420	480	70	20	10	22,300
10	Binder Dijker Otte	400	84	316	65	30	5	9,000
11	Grant Thornton Intl	340	137	203		n.a.		15,000[b]
12	Howarth & Howarth Intl	247	125	122		n.a.		7,000
13	Dunwoody, Robson, McGladry & Pullen	220	122	98		n.a.		4,500
14	Fox Moore Intl	218	91	127		n.a.		5,949
15	Spicer & Oppenheim	170	28	142		n.a.		5,837

Source: International Accounting Bulletin (December 1983).

a. MAS: Management Advisory Services.

b. Estimated by IAB.

Table 3–5. Gross Income of Transnational and Other Advertising Agencies, by Regions in Selected Countries, 1977.

	Transnational Agencies		Other Agencies		Total	
	Millions of Dollars	Percentage	Millions of Dollars	Percentage	Millions of Dollars	Percentage
Developed Countries	780.0	86.7	811.4	91.1	1,591.4	88.8
Southern Europe	16.7	1.9	11.4	1.3	28.1	1.6
Africa and Middle East	6.6	0.7	5.3	0.6	11.9	0.7
Latin America and Caribbean	75.4	8.4	51.8	5.8	127.2	7.1
Asia	22.4	2.5	10.8	1.2	33.2	1.8
Total	901.1	100.0	890.7	100.0	1,791.8	100.0

Source: U.N. Center on Transnational Corporations, *Transnational Corporations in Advertising,* Document ST-CT-8 (New York: United Nations, 1979). p. 8.

Note: Based on *Advertising Age* figures on gross income of 722 advertising agencies operating in 68 countries.

Developed countries: Australia, Austria, Belgium, Canada, Denmark, Federal Republic of Germany, Finland, France, Italy, Japan, Netherlands, New Zealand, Norway, Puerto Rico, South Africa, Sweden, Switzerland, United Kingdom.

Southern Europe: Greece, Malta, Portugal, Spain, Turkey, Yugoslavia.

Africa and Middle East: Egypt, Ghana, Kenya, Morocco, Nigeria, Sierra Leone; Iran, Israel, Kuwait, Lebanon.

Latin America and Caribbean: Argentina, Brazil, Chile, Colombia, Costa Rica, Ecuador, El Salvador, Guatemala, Honduras, Mexico, Nicaragua, Panama, Paraguay, Peru, Uruguay, Venezuela; Barbados, Bermuda, Curacao, Dominican Republic, Jamaica, Trinidad.

Asia: Hong Kong, India, Indonesia, Malaysia, Pakistan, Republic of Korea, Singapore, Sri Lanka, Thailand, Philippines.

Table 3–6. Thirty Largest Advertising Agencies Ranked by 1983 Worldwide Gross Income ($ millions).

World Rank	Agency	Gross Income World	Gross Income U.S.	U.S. Rank	Rank outside U.S.	Gross Income outside U.S.
1	(Jap) Dentsu	437.7	0.0	—	1	437.7
2	(USA) Young & Rubicam	414.0	274.4	1	8	139.6
3	(USA) Ted Bates Worldwide	388.0	244.4	2	5	143.6
4	(USA) J. Walter Thompson	378.8	189.9	5	3	188.9
5	(USA) Ogilvy & Mather	345.8	204.1	3	7	141.7
6	(USA) McCann Erickson	298.8	95.4	13	2	203.4
7	(USA) BBDO Intl	289.0	199.0	4	11	90.0
8	(UK) Saatchi & Saatchi, Compton	253.3	110.9	10	6	142.4
9	(USA) Leo Burnett	216.5	135.0	8	14	81.5
10	(USA) Foote Cone & Belding	208.4	158.9	6	19	49.5
11	(USA) Doyle Dane Bernbach	199.0	146.0	7	18	53.0
12	(USA) SSC&B Lintas	197.1	67.8	22	9	129.3
13	(USA) Grey Advertising	183.5	125.1	9	17	58.4
14	(USA) D'Arcy McManus Masius	181.1	91.6	15	13	89.5
15	(Jap) Hakuhodo	180.2	0.0	—	4	180.2
16	(USA) Benton & Bowles	144.3	98.1	12	21	46.2
17	(USA) Marschalk Campbell Ewald	133.0	99.5	11	24	33.5
18	(USA) Dancer Fitzgerald Sample	113.1	94.1	14	n.a.	19.0
19	(USA) NW Ayer	97.4	83.2	18	n.a.	14.2
20	(USA) Needham, Harper & Steers	94.2	77.9	19	n.a.	16.3
21	(USA) Wells, Rich & Greene	92.7	91.0	16	n.a.	1.7
22	(FR) Eurocom Intl	90.0	0.0	—	11	90.0
23	(USA) William Esty	84.8	84.8	17	—	0.0
24	(Fr) Publicis Intermarco Farner	82.1	3.0	n.a.	15	79.1
25	(Fr) Havas Conseil Masteller	75.0	27.0	33	20	48.0
26	(USA) Bozell & Jacobs	74.4	73.5	20	n.a.	0.9
27	(USA) Kenyon & Eckhardt	60.5	45.0	25	n.a.	15.5
28	(Jap) Daiko Advertising	59.8	0.0	—	16	59.8
29	(USA) Ketchum Communications	55.2	46.8	24	n.a.	8.4
30	(USA) Cunningham & Walsh	52.7	52.7	23	n.a.	0.0

Source: Medias (Paris), Oct. 8, 1984.

Table 3–7. Foreign Branch Offices of Selected ACME Member Firms, 1961, 1970, and 1980.

	Number of Firms in Sample	Number of Firms with Foreign Branch Offices and Number of Foreign Branch Offices					
		1961		1970		1980	
		Firms	Offices	Firms	Offices	Firms	Offices
New York firms	25	3	3	15	62	12	73
Chicago firms	9	1	1	5	23	5	32
Philadelphia firms	5	0	0	1	10	2	34

Source: Directories of the Association of Management Consulting Firms. From Thierry J. Noyelle, *The Coming of Age of Management Consulting: Implications for New York City,* Report to New York City's Office of Economic Development, 1984, p. 33.

Table 3–8.   Twenty Largest U.S. Management Consulting Firms, 1978, Ranked by Sales ($ millions).

Rank	Firm	Location	Worldwide Revenues
1	Booz Allen & Hamilton	New York	150
2	SRI	Palo Alto, Cal.	123
3	Arthur D. Little	Cambridge, Mass.	121
4	Arthur Andersen, MAS[a]	New York	114
5	McKinsey & Co.	New York	100
6	Coopers & Lybrand, MAS	Philadelphia	83
7	Touche Ross, MAS	New York	72
8	Peat Marwick, MAS	New York	70
9	Towers, Perrin, Forster & Crosby	New York	60
10	Arthur Young, MAS	New York	53
11	Ernst & Whinney, MAS	Cleveland	51
12	Hay Associates	Philadelphia	42
13	Reliance Group	New York	42
14	Price Waterhouse, MAS	New York	33
15	A.T. Kearney	Chicago	30
16	Boston Consulting Group	Cambridge, Mass.	27
17	Science Management	Philadelphia	25
18	Stanley	Muscatine, Iowa	25
19	A.H. Hansen	Chicago	25
20	Kurt Salomon Associates	New York	17

Source: Consultant News, *A Cross Section of the Management Consulting Industry* (Fitzwilliam, N.H.: Kennedy & Kennedy Inc., 1979), p. 8.

a. Sales shown are estimates of the sales of the MAS divisions of the large accounting firms.

Table 3–3 shows the worldwide distribution of the offices of the world's thirteen largest accounting firms in 1982. As with Arthur Andersen, this table suggests that the largest accounting firms have already established extensive networks of offices in North America and Europe, while their presence remains somewhat more scattered elsewhere. Six of the nine largest firms already have a total of over 350 offices worldwide.

In accounting the relationship between firms and their clients remains largely based on the certified and financial audits needed by both parent companies and their subsidiaries, either to meet statutory requirements or in advance of capital funding. In

Table 3–9. Foreign Offices of the 100 Largest U.S. Law Firms, 1965, 1978, and 1984.

	1965	1978	1984
Number of firms	100	100	100
Number of firms with foreign offices	22	33	46
Location of offices			
Paris	18	17	17
London	2	21	28
Brussels	3	6	5
Other European cities	3	9	9
Riyadh	0	0	4
Other Middle Eastern cities	0	1	4
Hong Kong	0	6	11
Singapore	0	1	6
Tokyo	1	3	4
Other Asian cities	0	4	8
Other cities	4	8	9

Source: "National Law Firms Survey," *National Law Journal*, various years.

1985 Deloitte, Haskins & Sells estimated that the firm was employing nearly 1,400 full-time people worldwide just to audit General Motors.[8] Granted that GM was then the world's largest multinational industrial company, this observation nevertheless underscores the fact that the largest accounting firms have themselves become very large organizations. By 1985 five of the nine largest firms were billion-dollar businesses, and each of the nine largest firms employed over 20,000 employees (see Table 3–4).

As they internationalized, large accounting firms had to comply with the requirement of most countries that branch offices be set up in partnership with locally licensed accountants. As a result, large accounting firms expanded principally by joining forces with existing local accounting partnerships, which they then brought under a more or less binding federating structure called an "affiliation" (see Chapter 4). Typically, an affiliation structure provides a legal framework under which certain training and development costs can be shared among

Table 3–10. Twenty Largest U.S. Law Firms, 1984, Ranked by Number of Lawyers.

Rank	Firm	Location	Number of Lawyers	Number of Foreign Branch Offices
1	Baker & McKenzie	Chicago	704	25
2	Finley, Kumble, Wagner, Heine, Underberg, Manley & Casey	New York	462	0
3	Sidley & Austin	Chicago	449	6
4	Skadden, Arps, Slate, Meagher & Flom	New York	416	0
5	Gibson, Dunn & Crutcher	Los Angeles	405	3
6	Shearman & Sterling	New York	397	4
7	O'Melveny & Myers	Los Angeles	392	0
8	Jones, Day, Reavis & Pogue	Cleveland	386	0
9	Hyatt Legal Services	Kansas City	379	0
10	Pillsbury, Madison & Sutro	San Francisco	373	0
11	Morgan, Lewis & Bockius	Philadelphia	370	1
12	Vinson & Elkins	Houston	357	1
13	Fulbright & Jaworski	Houston	353	1
14	Davis, Polk & Wardell	New York	312	2
15	Squire, Sanders & Dempsey	Cleveland	308	1
16	Mayer, Brown & Platt	Chicago	307	1
17	Simpson,Thacher & Bartlett	New York	305	3
18	Weil, Gotshal & Manges	New York	293	0
19	Sullivan & Cromwell	New York	280	3
20	Paul, Weiss, Rifkind, Wharton & Garrison	New York	276	2

Source: "Annual Survey of the Nation's 100 Largest Law Firms," *National Law Journal* (1985).

affiliates, personnel can be exchanged, and a unique brand of accounting methods can be offered worldwide. In the most centralized affiliation, that of Arthur Andersen, all partners are members of a Geneva-based Société Coopérative in addition to being partners in their local partnership. The firm is somewhat of an exception, however, having expanded abroad by creating its own local partnerships rather than by absorbing others. This particular pattern of expansion partly explains why the firm has far fewer offices than other multinational firms. This situation also reflects the firm's particular market strategy of concentrating personnel in a few locations rather than decentralizing into many field locations.

The pressure to stay with large multinational clients is fundamental to understanding the pattern of international expansion. Mergers among affiliations often are driven by the need to expand smaller networks into larger ones if the needs of key clients are to be satisfied. For example, the 1957 merger of Coopers (U.K.), Lybrand (U.S.), and McDonald (Canada), which resulted in the creation of Coopers & Lybrand, was dictated in part by Lybrand's need to follow Ford in Europe and Coopers' to follow Unilever in North America. Lately, Coopers & Lybrand Europe has been expanding along the western coast of Africa, in part to keep up with Unilever's expansion in that part of the world. Most recently, partners in Number Five, Klynveld Main Goerdder (KMG), and Number Two, Peat Marwick Mitchell, have agreed to a merger that will create the world's largest accounting firm. The merger was driven in large part by KMG's realization that its relatively weak North American network was inhibiting its relationship with its major European clients.

This seemingly never-ending drive to build large international networks has resulted in a high degree of market concentration among the largest firms. In 1983 the world's nine largest firms controlled probably over one-third of the world's accounting business.[9] Among the top fifteen firms, only two were not Anglo-American–dominated creations: Number Five, Klynveld Main Goerdder, and Number Ten, Binder Dijker Otte (BDO), both having originated from the affiliation of continental European partnerships (see Table 3–4). As was just noted, today only BDO remains independent.

Advertising

In advertising as in accounting, close firm-client relationships have also influenced considerably the expansion of advertising firms throughout the world. In addition, in a sector in which two to three hundred advertisers—mostly firms producing consumer goods and services—generate perhaps 70 percent or more of all advertising dollars worldwide, the gain or loss of a large account by an advertising agency can quickly turn into a make-or-break situation, especially for medium-sized agencies.[10] For example, Euro-Advertising, a medium-sized European multinational advertising firm that had built its network during the late 1960s and early 1970s around the account of SEB, a major European manufacturer of kitchen equipment and household appliances, saw its network collapse when the SEB account shifted to Ogilvy. Today Euro-Advertising is a fully owned subsidiary of J. Walter Thompson, and is down from twelve agencies in Europe in the late 1970s to only five (one each in France, England, Italy, West Germany, and Greece).

By the late 1970s the internationalization of advertising was quite advanced. In a 1979 technical paper, the UN Center on Transnational Corporations estimated from data published by *Advertising Age* that, as of 1977, the market outside the United States was split almost equally between transnational agencies and local agencies, with the group of transnational agencies dominated at that time by approximately thirty highly competitive, large multinational agencies.[11] Nearly 90 percent of the advertising expenditures occurred in the developed economies of North America, Western Europe, and Japan (see Table 3–5). By 1983 the group of transnational agencies was largely dominated by American firms, with only seven non-American firms ranked among the world's top thirty firms—three French, three Japanese, and one British (see Table 3–6).

Management Consulting

Table 3–7 shows the internationalization of a sample of thirty-nine U.S. management consulting firm members of the Association of Management Consulting Firms (ACME), a close-knit group including a limited number of the largest and/or most prestigious independent management consulting firms (fewer than sixty members in 1984). This table shows a steady process of internationalization among firms in the sample throughout the 1960s and 1970s, with the number of firms with international offices growing from four with a total of four foreign offices among them in 1961 to nineteen firms with 139 foreign offices among them in 1980. Although not shown in Table 3–7, for the most part internationalization among management consulting firms meant opening offices in key cities of the developed economies of Western Europe and Japan, including London, Paris, Brussels, Frankfurt, Tokyo, and a few other locations. Compared to the far more developed networks found in accounting and advertising, this phenomenon reflects partly the nature of the firm-client relationship in management consulting, where contacts between consultants and clients may not be as frequent as they are in the other two industries.

Because the emergence of management consulting as a sizable industry is rather recent, its statistical tracking is relatively poor and documentation of which firms dominate different markets is difficult to obtain.[12] But it is usually assumed that U.S. management firms, including increasingly the MAS of the largest accounting firms, have a commanding lead both domestically and abroad. SRI, for example, has been a major consultant to several Japanese automobile manufacturers on worldwide market strategies. Arthur Andersen's MAS division is a strong player both in the United States and in Europe in financial service industries. In Japan, McKinsey has been very influential in computerization strategies among financial firms. In Chapter 6, we present limited, yet somewhat more rigorous, evidence of the influence of U.S. firms in the U.K. market.

Lacking a list of the top management consulting firms worldwide, Table 3–8 presents the list of the twenty largest firms in the United States as of 1978. Note that by 1978 the accounting firms played a major role in the management consulting industry, even though most only became seriously involved in that business by no earlier than the late 1960s.

Legal Services

Table 3–9 shows the pattern of internationalization among the 100 largest U.S. law firms, with the number of U.S. firms maintaining foreign offices growing from twenty-two firms with a total of thirty-one foreign offices among them in 1965 to forty-six firms with 105 foreign offices among them in 1984.

In contrast to accounting, advertising, or even management consulting firms, however, a different pattern of internationalization developed among law firms, for both market and regulatory reasons. Rather than being driven by relationships with major multinational industrial clients, law firms during the post–World War II period have tended to locate branch offices where major banks and financial institutions are found (see Table 3–8). This is so because financial institutions have become a principal source of referrals to law firms, and because legal work demanded in the preparation of financial and like documents has become a staple for many large business law firms. In addition, regulatory constraints have played a greater role in shaping the internationalization of large law firms than is the case with other business services.[13] From the point of view of large business law firms, internationalization has meant first and foremost breaking through regulatory constraints in a few large international banking centers (see Chapter 5).

Owing to their roles as major financial centers, London and Paris became Western Europe's two major legal centers during the 1960s and 1970s.[14] Brussels was also able to profit from the growth of legal activity during the same period, a growth generated in that city by the presence of the European Commission. In contrast, West Germany did not capture a share of the legal activity commensurate with the importance of its economy and the size of its banks. A highly restrictive regulatory environment locked out foreign firms, closed out options for the emergence of large local firms, and confined the bulk of legal work to only a few of the large in-house legal departments of the large German banks. Paris benefited from West Germany's relative protectionism in legal services as Paris-based firms picked up some of the German business. Paris also profited from its traditional links to the Middle East, North Africa, and French Africa as a number of firms developed expertise relevant to those regions, for which demand grew in the late 1970s. Finally, Paris benefited from the growth in international arbitration activity under the auspices of the International Chamber of Commerce headquartered in that city. London, of course, capitalized primarily on its emergence as the center of the Eurodollar market.

In the Far East, linkages to the financial markets have again been a major consideration in the geographical expansion of multinational law firms in recent years. In addition, Hong Kong has recently benefited from its role as a gateway to the People's Republic of China as that country has begun reopening its economy to the rest of the world. Indeed, a number of multinational law firms have opened offices in Hong Kong recently to ensure that they be grandfathered before the colony reverts to China's control. By comparison to Hong Kong, which has been relatively liberal in its treatment of foreign law firms, Japan has proved to be a more difficult place to enter (see Chapter 5).

Elsewhere in the Far East, Singapore has also become a favorite location for large, mostly American and British, law firms. Some law firms as well as other business service firms have also looked toward Australia as a possible major center for business services because of its special connection to both Asian and Anglo-American cultures. This perception has been reinforced in recent years by sizable investment in that country by the Japanese and lately by the South Koreans and Hong Kong Chinese. In the legal field, however, this hope has yet to become a reality. A splintered court system in Australia has prevented, thus far, the emergence of any one of the large Australian cities as the dominant legal center.

As was the case in management consulting, we were unable to find a comprehensive listing of the world's largest business law firms. However, it is usually assumed that the industry is dominated by large U.S. business law firms and U.K. solicitor firms. Geographically, the U.S. firms dominate both the New York and U.S. markets, while the U.K. firms dominate the London market. The legal market is somewhat more competitive in Paris, Brussels, Hong Kong, or Singapore, but remains highly protected in Tokyo and Frankfurt. We return to this issue in Chapter 6. For lack of better data, Table 3–10 presents a list of the twenty largest U.S. law firms in 1984, ranked by number of lawyers (including partners and associates). With only thirteen of the top twenty firms maintaining even one foreign office in 1984, it is clear that involvement in international business law through establishment abroad remains limited.

FUTURE MARKETS

As they were asked to assess the future of their industries, most executives interviewed for this study argued that new business opportunities would come about in three principal ways: by opening new geographical markets; by broadening the range of customers; and by diversifying the scope of activities.

While parts of Western Europe may not have yet reached a level of market development similar to that found in North America, most executives tend to regard those two major markets as fairly mature and look to other areas of the world for new, relatively underdeveloped markets. Typically, these include the newly industrialized countries (NICs)—South Korea, Taiwan, Hong Kong, Malaysia, Singapore, Indonesia and Brazil— and also India and China.

With the exception of Brazil, Latin American countries tend to be seen as lackluster performers, troubled by their huge debt; Middle Eastern countries as potentially large markets but very unstable at the moment; and African countries, with a few exceptions, as still too underdeveloped.

In countries in which markets for large corporate customers already are well developed, the emphasis is on both the diversification of activities and the expansion of the customer base. Typically, small and medium-sized corporate customers, individual consumers, and public-sector agencies are seen as prime new clients. Market situations vary widely however. In accounting, for example, legally mandated certified audits are fairly new in some of the southern European countries (Italy and Spain), and there is still much competition for large corporate customers.

Throughout most of continental Europe there remains a considerably undertapped market among corporate middle-market firms. Prior to the recent introduction of changes in the national legislation of EC member countries following the issuance of several European Economic Community (EEC) directives in the early 1980s, middle-market European firms were most often not required to issue certified accounts. In contrast, in the United Kingdom and the United States, where the market for certified audits is already saturated, the emphasis has shifted to selling a broader range of service and to reaching deeper into the market. In terms of individual consumers and public-sector clients, opportunities for expansion are likewise seen as varying, depending on countries.

This leads us to the third major way in which business service firms are attempting to develop new business opportunities—diversification. The trend is particularly noticeable among accounting firms, but can be found in other fields as well.

In the market for business customers, accounting firms have been very aggressive in expanding the scope of their offerings in areas of tax services and management advisory services. As shown in Table 3–4, large accounting firms already generate 25 percent or more of their worldwide gross income from those newer areas. In a number of European countries where *conseils juridiques* are loosely regulated, several of the large accounting firms have in-house *conseil juridique* departments that can advise on legal matters. In advertising, a firm such as Saatchi & Saatchi, Compton—which has now raced ahead to the Number One spot—is stressing its ability to offer a very wide scope of advertising and marketing services ranging from corporate image (through its Philadelphia-based subsidiary, Hay Associates) to market research and polling (through its Connecticut-based subsidiary, Yankelovitch) and straight advertising services through either the Saatchi & Saatchi, Compton network or the Ted Bates network, now a subsidiary (see Chapter 6).[15]

In the market for individual consumers, a big push is under way among some accountants and lawyers to pursue more aggressively the market for asset management services for high–net worth individuals. The argument is that, in today's new world of finance, characterized by vastly expanding investment opportunities for individual investors, there is an enormous but underserved market for tax and investment services for high–net worth individuals. While competition is bringing many new actors into the same field—including commercial banks, stock brokers, *notaires* (in continental Europe), lawyers, accountants, and many others—a number of accounting and law firms see new opportunities for growth in these areas. As recently as 1985, one U.K.-based accounting firm considered taking over a brokerage house to create some synergies to serve this particular market. While this particular firm did not follow through, many business service firms in the United Kingdom see financial deregulation as an opportunity to find new niches.

In the end, many of these developments are similar to those taking place in other service industries today, especially financial industries. They underscore the desire by some to develop so-called service supermarkets, in which firms attempt to refocus and reorganize by delivering a broad range of services to targeted market segments instead of a few services to a very wide market. However, the extent to which such a transformation may take place will be determined in part by national regulatory constraints, since it may necessitate bringing together different areas of professional expertise that, under current regulations, are not allowed to join forces.

CONCLUSIONS: NETWORKS AND THE FORMATION OF COMPARATIVE ADVANTAGES

The information presented in this chapter points to several critical factors underlying the creation of comparative advantages by large multinational business service organizations and suggests important questions regarding the nature of competition in some of the business service markets. Clearly, questions of competition in various markets must be assessed, because answers to such questions are likely to have major implications for future negotiations. The competition issue is taken up in detail in Chapters 6 and 7. Here, we simply review the issue of comparative advantages.

Undoubtedly, a principal objective behind the development of large multinational networks includes both the search for greater economies of scale and scope as well as the desire to raise costs of entry and competition for others in the market. The strategy used to reach these goals is the creation of special linkages, both geographical and institutional, that encourage clients to use an ever expanding diversity of services from the same supplier while making it costly for these clients to switch over to competitors or to multiply the number of their suppliers.

Perhaps more than any other factor today, the need to pay for the resources demanded by the information technology revolution explains the need for scale economies. New information technology is playing an increasingly major role in integrating the various affiliates within an organization through growing interoffice flows of information and, more importantly, by changing the nature of the services delivered to clients. Significantly, the costs of the new information technology are associated not so much with hardware as they are with the development of new products and the training of personnel. Estimates of R&D and training costs in the range of 15 to 25 percent of gross revenues are common in the accounting industry. In the opinion of one interviewee, the burden is likely to be felt particularly by medium-sized firms:

> Years ago in the United States we used to have a three-tier industry with a few large accounting firms, a larger number of medium-sized firms, and numerous small firms. We have seen a process of integration and mergers that basically has resulted in a market now characterized by a number of very large firms, still a large number of small firms, but very few medium-sized firms. The latter have been forced out. In my opinion, the process is going to continue but now increasingly on the world scale.

While forces pushing toward greater scale may not be as strong in the other three sectors as they are in accounting, evidence nevertheless exists that similar tendencies are at work in advertising and management consulting.

Economies of scope are also an important factor behind the formation of large networks. In services, perhaps even more so than in goods, clients have very limited means for assessing the quality and usefulness of the product that they are purchasing until they have indeed done so. Service firms must invest considerable resources in building their reputations and in enhancing their clients' trust in the professionalism of their work. They may need to spend a considerable number of non-billable hours with prospective clients negotiating, discussing, and explaining the firm's service offering. This is the impetus behind the attempts of service firms to recoup some of these costs by trying to expand the scope of their offerings, a trend often further reinforced by the maturing of traditional markets.

Putting together greater scale and greater scope assumes that the firm is able to establish unique linkages with clients that competitors may not be able to reproduce.

In the accounting industry, perhaps the most important linkage has become the financial audit, which the firm needs in advance of raising new capital. As a result, the traditional linkages between the Big 8 Anglo-American firms and New York-based or London-based financial institutions is giving those firms a formidable comparative advantage over other accounting firms, at least in the accounting service market for large multinational clients. One French accountant, whose firm had just joined one of the Big 8 told us in an interview: "From the point of view of a multinational firm, having one's books audited by a Big 8 means interest rates several points lower on Wall Street." Furthermore, once a large accounting affiliation has attracted the account of a particular firm, the accountant is in an advantageous position to expand his offerings because, as one lawyer put it: "The accountant is in and out of his customer's premises on a weekly basis and benefits from having a unique access to the customer's books. In turn, this puts him in a remarkably favorable position to suggest additional tax or management consulting services." In addition, the accountant benefits from the fact that, since much of the financial information that he handles is privileged, switching accountants and relying on too many service suppliers increases the client's risks of doing business in a world where competitors, raiders, or other potential adversaries are all seeking to obtain such information.

In the advertising industry, the most important current linkages between advertisers and advertising agencies have to do with the concepts of "total marketing" and "global advertising." Total marketing implies that advertisers look at their promotional budgets in their totality, that is, in terms of the trade-offs among advertising expenditures, public relations dollars, discount campaigns (for example, coupons in the food industry, cash rebates in the automobile industry), and other promotional approaches. With global advertising, multinational advertisers attempt to target markets on a customer segment basis rather than on a geographical basis and to project a unique image to a particular target segment across borders.

To offer total marketing, advertising agencies must be able to offer concurrent and complementary services—market research, advertising, public relations, and so forth. To offer global advertising, advertising firms must be able to develop global advertising concepts and must offer a worldwide network of agencies to carry out local campaigns consistent with such concepts. To a great extent, total marketing and global advertising means getting involved in product strategy, if not corporate strategy. Such involvment can in turn make advertising firms privy to confidential information, making it costly for clients to switch over to competitors.

In management consulting, the dynamics of the industry seem to be dictated more and more by what is happening in both accounting and advertising. Thus, some management consulting firms specializing in strategy, market research, market surveys, and the like are now feeling growing competition from advertising firms, while others are feeling it from accountants.

In the case of legal services, the capacity to establish exclusive linkages with clients remains probably much weaker than in advertising or accounting. Nevertheless, the importance of the relationship between legal services and banking services seems to suggest that the historical linkages between certain U.S.

law firms and New York-based financial institutions, and between U.K. solicitor firms and London-based financial institutions, are giving those American and British firms an important comparative advantage over competitors from other countries.

Clearly, the strength of the linkages between users and providers is likely to vary from one service sector to another. It is likely to also be influenced in part by the institutional constraints that are placed on the activities of service firms in various countries. Ultimately, however, trade negotiators may need to determine how high are the barriers to entry in various sectors and what are the implications for sector-specific negotiations. We return to these issues in the last two chapters, after having assessed the nature of national restrictions on the operations of multinational service firms in the next two chapters.

NOTES

1. For a history of early developments in the accounting industry, see Robert Cohen, "The Internationalization of Capital and U.S. Cities," (Ph.D. dissertation, New School for Social Research, 1974).
2. Thierry J. Noyelle, *The Coming of Age of Management Consulting: Implications for New York City*, Report to New York City's Office of Economic Development, 1984.
3. Henri Schwamm and Patrizio Merciai, *The Multinationals and the Services*, IRM Multinational Report No. 6, October-December 1985 (New York: John Wiley and Sons); see also Thierry J. Noyelle, "Economic Transformation," in Marvin E. Wolfgang and Ralf Widner, eds., *Revitalizing the Industrial City*, Annals of the American Academy of Political and Social Science, vol. 488 (Beverly Hills: Sage Publications, 1986).
4. Thomas M. Stanback, Peter J. Bearse, Thierry J. Noyelle, and Robert A. Karasek, *Services/The New Economy* (Totowa, N.J.: Rowman and Allanheld, 1981).
5. See Andrew Leyson, Peter Daniels, and Nigel Thrift, "Large Accountancy Firms in the U.K.: Operational Adaptation and Spatial Development" (Working paper, St. David's University

College, Lampter, and University of Liverpool, March 1987) for a treatment of the British case.

6. Peter Daniels, Andrew Leyhson, and Nigel Thrift, "U.K. Producer Services: The International Dimension" (Working paper, St. David's University College, Lampter, and University of Liverpool, August 1986).

7. Arthur Andersen & Co., *The First Sixty Years: 1913–1973* (Chicago: Arthur Anderson & Co., 1974); see also Frank A. Rossi, "Government Impediments and Professional Constraints on the Operations of International Accounting Organizations," *University of Chicago Legal Forum 1*, no. 1 (November 1986).

8. Daniels, et al., "U.K. Producer Services," p. 14.

9. *International Accounting Bulletin* (December 1983).

10. *Advertising Age* (various years).

11. UN Center on Transnational Corporations, *Transnational Corporations in Advertising*, Document ST-CT-8 (New York: United Nations, 1979).

12. For a historical analysis of the development of management consulting, see Noyelle, *The Coming of Age of Management Consulting*.

13. See Sydney M. Cone III, "Government Trade Policy and the Professional Regulation of Foreign Lawyers," *University of Chicago Legal Forum 1*, no. 1 (November 1986).

14. Christopher R. Brown, "Europe's Top Lawyers and Law Firms," *International Financial Law Review* (October 1983).

15. See Saatchi & Saatchi, *Fiscal Year 1986 Annual Report*, as reported in *New York Times*, 5 Dec. 1986, Business section.

4

IMPEDIMENTS TO TRADE IN BUSINESS SERVICES
Principal Restrictions

In this and the next chapter, we examine impediments to international trade in business services, retaining the broadest possible concept of trade—one that encompasses both transborder trade and establishment trade. Thus, we focus on impediments applying to either one or both situations.

Our interviews with executives, managers, and practicing professionals in the fields of accounting, law, advertising, and management consulting helped us to identify eight areas of restrictions impeding the international expansion of business service firms. These were: (1) restrictions on local ownership and on the right of establishment, (2) restrictions on international payment transfers, (3) restrictions on the mobility of personnel, (4) restrictions on technology transfer, (5) restrictions on transborder data flow, (6) procurement policies, (7) local restrictions on the business scope of firms, and (8) restrictions on the use of a firm's name. While this list was developed through an exhaustive analysis of information collected through our own interviews, it is worth noting that it is quite similar to a list developed recently by Frank A. Rossi, a managing partner at Arthur Andersen. Rossi's list comes from an in-depth survey of the trade impediments faced by twenty-seven of his firm's foreign affiliates. It is also similar to a list recently developed by *The Conference Board*, based on a questionnaire survey of 227 service multinationals, including nineteen business service firms.[1]

In this chapter, we review the eight areas of restrictions identified above as they apply broadly to the four business services under analysis. In the next chapter, we take a closer look at restrictions on personnel licensing and on the right of establishment as they apply to the two licensed professions, accounting and law.

RESTRICTIONS ON THE RIGHT OF ESTABLISHMENT

In most market economies, advertising and management consulting are unregulated industries, which means that countries place neither "natural monopoly" restrictions nor licensing requirement restrictions on the right of establishment of foreign firms as they usually do for the legal and accounting industries. Restrictions on the right of establishment of foreign advertising or management consulting firms are thus attributable primarily to the ways in which individual countries exercise national sovereignty over foreign direct investment and, in particular, to the requirements each country places on local ownership. In some cases, the same ownership restrictions also apply to accounting and legal services; in many cases, however, restrictions on ownership are more stringent for lawyers and accountants than they are for other service areas.

Obviously, it it beyond the scope of this study to develop a complete panorama of the principal rules that major countries or groups of countries apply to the regulation of foreign direct investment. Nevertheless, a few words may be useful to indicate how such restrictions tend to be perceived by firms in this study's four sectors.

Typically, advertising and management consulting firms are able to expand abroad by opening or buying local agencies in combinations involving partial or total ownership of their local affilitates' capital. In some highly restrictive countries, however, advertising and management consulting firms may not be allowed to own capital in local establishments. In that case, they usually try to operate through a system of "network affiliation" that links them to locally owned firms via a set of preferential relationships involving no exchange of capital. In the least structured affiliations, the extent of preferential relationships is limited to straightforward referral of clients. In the most structured affiliations, such relationships may involve the sharing of business assignments, transfers of technology among members of the affiliation, shared training programs, shared R&D work, joint methods and procedures, and the like.

While network affiliations are infrequent in advertising, their use has increased among management consultants. Network affiliations have given consulting firms a faster and cheaper way of broadening their international reach and competing with the MAS divisions of the accounting firms than would have been possible through de novo growth or through the purchase of locally established consulting firms.[2] The situation is somewhat different in legal and accounting services. European business law firms, organized mostly as single-office operations, rely extensively on loose network affiliations to provide each other with referrals. By comparison, American and British law firms—likely to be more internationalized than their European counterparts—have tended to move abroad by opening their own branch offices, often under restrictive conditions. Finally, network affiliation is the rule among accounting firms. Typically, however, accounting affiliations are highly structured networks with formal legal arrangements allowing for extensive sharing of resources among affiliate members and extensive integration of members within the affiliation.

Given the practice among advertising and management consulting firms to expand abroad mostly or partly through branches and subsidiaries, executives in these firms normally regard Western Europe as "wide open." By comparison, they regard Canada, Australia, and many Latin American countries as relatively restrictive.

While Canada grants minority interests fairly easily (ranging from 35 percent to 49 percent), its Foreign Investment Review Board demands a rigid and extensive review of firms that want to gain a majority interest.[3] Those who seek to acquire a majority interest need to demonstrate that such investment is in the interest of Canada and will result in both increased local employment and R&D.

In Latin America, restrictions became commonplace in the wake of the Andean Pact, although various countries interpret the pact differently. That agreement entered into force on October 16, 1969 and was later changed to the Cartagena Agreement. The agreement was adopted by the governments of Bolivia, Chile, Colombia, Ecuador, Peru, and Venezuela. Chile withdrew in 1976.[4] In Colombia, Venezuela, and Peru, foreign firms are not allowed to hold equity in local firms, except for those firms that benefited from a grandfather clause because they had invested in these countries prior to the signing of the pact. While Colombia and Venezuela permit such grandfathered firms to maintain a 20 percent equity interest in local firms, Chile allows such firms to hold a 35 percent minority interest. In most of these countries, then, advertising and management consulting firms must operate through minority holdings or through loose associations with local firms. Only in Brazil can foreigners hold a majority interest in local firms, but the country puts drastic restrictions on the repatriation of profits and capital.

In the Pacific area, restrictions on local ownership differ from country to country. Japan sets no restrictions. Australia does, but according to one executive, that country is interested in attracting non-Japanese foreign investment. India, Malaysia, Indonesia, and South Korea favor local ownership. For that matter, Indonesia and South Korea often prohibit equity positions and allow only management contracts.

On the whole, advertising firms appear to be the most sensitive to many of these restrictions. For the most part, management consulting firms thus far have rarely ventured beyond Western Europe ("wide open"). Only to the extent that some management consulting firms have begun moving beyond Europe have they been confronted with more restrictive environments, usually in the Middle East (at times, very restrictive) or in the Pacific area.

In law and accounting, as already noted, restrictions have differed owing to the commingling of restrictions on the right of establishment and on the licensing of foreign professionals. These restrictions are examined in the next chapter. Let us simply note here that in law—except for a very few large firms that are attempting to build an extensive, worldwide presence—international expansion has meant coping principally with restrictions in the few major locations where international business law is practiced—namely, London, Paris, and Brussels in Western Europe, Riyadh and Abu Dhabi in the Middle East, and Tokyo, Hong Kong, and Singapore in the Pacific area.

On balance, multinational accounting firms seem not to have met with many restrictions thus far, with the exception of a few countries, mostly in the Middle East and the Pacific and Asian areas. While most countries demand that local affiliates be set up as national partnerships, most allow these local partnerships to join international affiliations. To repeat, we return to this issue in the next chapter.

RESTRICTIONS ON INTERNATIONAL PAYMENTS

A second group of restrictions faced by business service firms stems from limitations on international transfer payments that are applied by most countries to control capital flows and foreign exchange.

In addition to the transfer of funds required for start-up investments, international payments are needed for two main reasons. First, international payments enable local offices to share investment costs in new products and services, costs of joint training, and other developmental costs, achieving economies of scale and scope on a multinational basis. Accounting firms, for example, must rely on extensive training of their personnel. As noted in the previous chapter, training costs in the range of 15 to 25 percent of the firm's revenues are not unusual among large accounting firms. But while some training of junior accountants is often done at the local level, or is shared by several agencies within the same country, training of senior accountants, account managers, and partners usually requires bringing together people from various countries into one or several central locations. Indeed, a main purpose of such training is to develop shared standards, techniques, procedures, and, perhaps even most importantly, a shared "company culture" among members of the same international affiliation.

Second, international payments are needed for the intrafirm billing of costs incurred by one branch office in contributing to an assignment carried out by another. This may happen, for example, in the audit of the consolidated accounts of a multinational client; in the preparation of a legal document that requires expertise from more than one office in more than one country; in the handling of a multinational advertising campaign or consulting assignment; and in other similar situations.

There are two principal ways in which international payments are restricted. One formula does not permit deduction of international intrafirm payments for income tax purposes, while the other limits the value of such transfers to a direct proportion of capital investment. Since most services are labor-intensive businesses, this particular rule tends to put these industries at a disadvantage.

RESTRICTIONS ON THE MOBILITY OF PERSONNEL

Restrictions placed by national governments on the mobility of non-nationals may constitute another type of impediment. The problem often is complicated by the different but nevertheless closely related forms that such restrictions may take. These include: visa restrictions, both on travel and immigration; restrictions on the right to practice; and restrictions on the right of establishment.

Executives, managers, and professionals from multinational business service firms typically need to travel for intrafirm transfers of technology, skill formation of branch employees, and business assignments. As long as those needs can be met through short-term travel and do not involve the direct conduct of business, few restrictions are usually encountered. One exception is the case of countries that restrict the right of their own nationals to travel abroad, limiting the firm's capacity to train local employees by sending them abroad.

As soon as the purpose of travel involves the conduct of business—such as servicing a short-term assignment, developing a business assignment to be carried out later in the home office, or more importantly, assigning foreign nationals to another country's branch office or affiliate—visa and work permit restrictions may become more serious. This is the case particularly, although not exclusively, among the licensed professions, since most countries link the right to practice to residence (sometimes citizenship) requirements and certification requirements. Visas are issued usually on the basis of whether or not individuals can meet domestic licensing restrictions.

Furthermore, many countries, including the United States, restrict the capacity of licensed professionals to practice their trade on a transient basis and require them to practice within the confine of a local establishment, which is itself subject to restrictions. These issues are explored in detail in the next chapter.

RESTRICTIONS ON TECHNOLOGY TRANSFER

Business service firms face some restrictions on technology transfers that, in the case of businesses that are human capital–intensive, often take the form of restrictions on the international movement of personnel. Presumably, this ensures that local firms are given the opportunity to create locally some of the technology they need, including opportunities to develop new operating procedures and to train personnel in the use of those new procedures.

In addition, countries may use high tariffs to restrict the import of technical and training publications. Some accounting firms complain of tariffs placed on the import of software. While few countries place restrictions on the import and local use of printed advertising copy material, many forbid the local use of imported advertising videos. Many countries see the production of videos as an important way to fuel the development of their movie and television industries—by creating local employment and by keeping their industries up-to-date on the newest technologies.

RESTRICTIONS ON TRANSBORDER DATA FLOWS

None of the firms in the four industries surveyed for this study cited restrictions on transborder data flows as a major problem, largely because none of them depend in any significant way on such flows. For most firms, the use of transborder data flows is occasional, be it lawyers' needs to access legal case data base services or the infrequent international transfer of data by accountants. It is unclear whether or not the increasing computerization within these industries will change the need for transborder trade of services by increasing the tradability of services, because there seems to be almost as equally powerful market forces pulling firms toward the use of distributed data processing as toward the use of centralized data processing systems. Obviously, this situation may be quite different in other business services such as engineering and architecture, where the use of centralized, computer-assisted design has become extensive. We return to this issue in Chapter 6.

NATIONAL PROCUREMENT RESTRICTIONS

Most countries, including the United States, discriminate by administrative rule or simply de facto against foreign business service firms by channeling the business of public-sector agencies, public authorities, and firms from the nationalized sectors to domestic service firms. In countries where these sectors represent a large share of the economy, this practice may be quite significant.

In advertising, for example, many French firms have long made it a practice to channel their business to French advertising firms, primarily to the Eurocom International, Havas Conseil, and Publicis networks—which together with their many local affiliates still control somewhere between 40 and 50 percent of the domestic market. Similarly, Japanese firms have long favored the services of Japanese advertising firms.

Bavishi and Wyman, in *Who Audits the World*, note that several countries have had an unwritten rule that the accounting business of the public and nationalized sectors should go to local partnerships.[5] In both Japan and again France, public- and private-sector firms alike have consistently favored local accounting firms, although this may now be changing in the French case (see Chapter 6).

In management consulting, similar unwritten rules appear to have been in effect in some of the European countries, at least in the late 1960s and early 1970s.[6]

How restrictive such practices have been in the past may be debatable, given the often very large market shares that U.S. business service firms have been able to secure for themselves in many countries. Indeed, "buy-national" practices seem to have come more often as a reaction to the great strides made by foreign firms in local markets and an attempt to avoid total domination of local markets by a few foreign firms than as an a priori attempt to exclude foreign firms from participation in the local market. Nevertheless, such restrictions are likely to become an important issue in future negotiations, and we return to that issue in Chapters 6 and 7.

RESTRICTIONS ON THE SCOPE OF BUSINESS

Business service firms complain of existing local rules that sometimes restrict the range of businesses they are allowed to enter. Often, however, the same restrictions apply to both domestic and foreign firms and simply reflect the way national governments decide to regulate some sectors. In continental Europe, for example, the certification of accounts and the preparation of accounts are two lines of business activity that by statute must be kept separated. However, large accounting firms usually handle this requirement quite simply—by establishing separate partnerships for each area.

In general, many countries do not allow partnerships of one licensed profession to either include or employ professionals from another licensed profession, except for their own internal use. In an era in which large professional business service firms are trying to grow through supermarket-style strategies that emphasize delivering a broad range of professional services tailored to particular market segments, rather than a few services to mass markets, such restrictions may understandably create problems for such firms.

As in the case of national restrictions on procurement, restrictions on the scope of business—be they specific to foreign firms or common to both domestic and foreign firms—are likely to be a major issue on the negotiating agenda. We also return to a discussion of this issue in Chapters 6 and 7.

RESTRICTIONS ON THE USE OF A FIRM'S NAME

Finally, a few individuals interviewed for this study complained of restrictions on the use of a firm's name. This assessment did not appear to be widely shared, however, and for that matter seemed somewhat contradicted by some of Bavishi and Wyman's findings for the accounting industry.[7]

In a series of tabulations presented in *Who Audits the World*, Bavishi and Wyman distributed the worldwide partners of the thirteen largest accounting firms according to the name under which they signed audits. Their detailed breakdown can be summarized into two main categories. In the first category, partners sign audits under the international name of the firm or under a name combining the international name with the name of a local partnership. In the second group, partners sign audits under a local name. The results are presented in Table 4–1.

Table 4–1. Percentage of Partners in the Twelve Largest Accounting Firms Using the Firm's International Name or a Local Name.

| | Partners Using: | | |
| | International | Local | Total Number of |
Firms	Name	Name	Partners
Arthur Andersen	99	1	1,493
Arthur Young	53	47	1,964
Binder Dijker Otte	1	99	920
Coopers & Lybrand	76	24	2,282
Deloitte Haskins & Sells	72	28	2,149
Ernst & Whinney	89	11	1,528
Grant Thornton Intl	—	100	1,206
Howarth & Howarth Intl	3	97	711
Klynveld Main Goerdder	—	100	2,308
Peat Marwick Mitchell	94	6	2,197
Price Waterhouse	94	6	1,728
Touche Ross	60	40	2,054
Total	59	41	20,540

Source: Vinod B. Bavishi and Harold E. Wyman, *Who Audits the World: Trends in the Worldwide Accounting Profession* (Storrs, CT: University of Connecticut Center for Transnational Accounting and Financial Research, 1983), pp. 30, 32.

Table 4–1 suggests that the use of the international name has as much to do with a firm's strategy or degree of internal development as with local restrictions. The second-tier firms and the two large European firms—BDO and KMG—use mostly local names. The Big 8 firms, Arthur Andersen, Peat Marwick Mitchell, and Price Waterhouse put a heavy emphasis on using the international name, while Coopers & Lybrand, Deloitte Haskins & Sells, and Touche Ross are more flexible in their use of local names. The data for Arthur Andersen, Peat Marwick Mitchell, and Price Waterhouse—where 99, 94, and 94 percent of the partners, respectively, sign audits under the international name—would hardly support an argument that restrictions on the use of a firm's international name are widespread and overwhelming.

CONCLUSIONS

The list of principal trade restrictions cited by firms in the four sectors in our study and examined in this chapter provides striking evidence of the commingling of restrictions involving transborder trade, investment trade, and personnel issues. In formulating both policy positions and negotiating strategies, negotiators will need to decide whether or not these should be dealt with separately or jointly and which are the most appropriate forums for dealing with each aspect of restrictions on service trade. We address some of these issues in Chapters 6 and 7, after taking a closer look at impediments specific to the licensed professions.

NOTES

1. See Frank A. Rossi, "Government Impediments and Professional Constraints on the Operations of International Accounting Organizations," *University of Chicago Legal Forum* 1, no. 1 (November 1986), and James R. Basche, "Eliminating Barriers to International Trade and Investment in Services," *The Conference Board*, Economic and Policy Analysis Program, Research Bulletin No. 200 (1986).
2. See Thierry J. Noyelle, *The Coming of Age of Management Consulting: Implications for New York City*, Report to New York City's Office of Economic Development, 1984.
3. See Canadian Foreign Investment Review Act of 1973–74. R.S.C., ch. 46; amended in 1976–77.
4. See Andean Subregional Integration Agreement, 8 Int'l. Legal Mat. 910 (September 1969).
5. Vinod B. Bavishi and Harold E. Wyman, *Who Audits the World: Trends in the Worldwide Accounting Profession* (Storrs, Conn.: 1983), University of Connecticut: Center for Transnational Accounting of Financial Research.
6. Noyelle, *The Coming of Age of Management Consulting*.
7. Bavishi and Wyman, *Who Audits the World*, chap. 7.

5

IMPEDIMENTS TO TRADE IN BUSINESS SERVICES
Restrictions on the Licensed Professions

As was noted in the previous chapter, professional business services face special problems as a result of licensing requirements that may have an impact on both the right of practice of individuals and the right of establishment of firms. This chapter reviews major licensing restrictions in the legal and accounting fields.

THE REGULATION OF LEGAL PRACTICE

A major part of the work of international lawyers involves the preparation of legal business documents and the resolution of conflicts that may arise in the course of business transactions. What complicates matters is that in today's world economy many business transactions are international by nature and can involve several legal systems at once. Attempts by lawyers to secure the right to practice outside their country of origin, however, raise thorny issues of licensing, citizenship requirements, grants of visas, and the right of establishment.

As has been mentioned previously, the nature of the relationship between lawyers and clients is such that international business lawyers and law firms have been concerned primarily with being able to operate in major financial/commercial centers—New York, Los Angeles, San Francisco, Chicago, and Dallas in this country; Paris, London, Hong Kong, Tokyo, and Singapore abroad—and possibly also in a few key administrative governmental centers—Brussels in Europe and Washington, D.C. in the United States.

In general, legal systems that have several categories of legal practitioners and that rest on narrow definitions of the practice of law, usually restricted to native law—as is the case in a number of West European countries—may be the most likely to provide niches for foreign practitioners. In contrast, systems with a single category of legal practitioners ("lawyers") who alone have the right to practice law, together with a broad definition of legal practice encompassing native and foreign law alike—as is true in the United States—may, in theory at least, be the most exclusionary of foreign legal practitioners. In addition, a lawyer's ability to practice in the courts may be far more important in countries where court litigation is central to the legal process than in those where legal codes play a far more extensive role.

In the following paragraphs we review the evolving arrangements that have developed over the years between foreign lawyers and national or state regulatory authorities in nine key international locations.[1]

France

Apart from its central geographic location in continental Europe and its extensive communications and transportation systems ("Along with Switzerland, one of the best telephone systems in Europe today," according to one lawyer, compared to the 1960s when "the United Kingdom phone system was by far the best"), the ease with which foreign lawyers were able to practice in France during the 1950s and 1960s goes far to explain the unique role that Paris developed after World War II. While a clause introduced in a 1971 law regulating legal professions in France has had the potential to make that country more restrictive, its impact thus far seems to have been limited. One source did mention the recent case of one U.S. law firm that had planned to open an office in Paris and had run into trouble. Unfortunately, we were unable to double-check that information. It is true, however, that parts of the French legal profession turned more protectionist during the 1970s and early 1980s than had been the case earlier.

The chief vehicle of France's earlier accommodation of foreign lawyers was the structure of the French legal profession—which is not unitary, like the American system, but divided into three major professions: *avocats, notaires,* and *conseils juridiques.* Law No. 71–1130, enacted on 31 December 1971, and subsequent executive orders (*décrets d'applications*) spelled out the boundaries of the three professions and made some changes in the previous system.[2]

Under the new law, the *avocats* retain their monopoly on practice in French civil and criminal courts, and the requirement of French citizenship is maintained. Changes were introduced that broaden the rights of association among *avocats* who, until the early 1970s, were highly restricted in their capacity to share work with one another. These changes were a contributing factor to the emergence of a sizable number of international *avocat* firms in the late 1970s and early 1980s, subsequently in direct competition with *conseil juridique* firms. (See Chapter 6.)

The *notaires* retain their monopoly over many recorded legal documents and their dominant role in trust and estate work. As with *avocats,* French citizenship remains a requirement.

Informally regulated until 1971, the *conseil juridique* was recognized as a separate profession under the new law, which also now provides for formal standards of education and training. The tradition was continued, however, of not requiring French citizenship, since legal counseling is not considered a part of the monopoly of the French bar or of the *Ordre des Notaires.*

Conseil juridique was the status under which business lawyers—both foreign and French—had traditionally operated: foreign lawyers because of their automatic exclusion from the other two professions, and French business lawyers because traditionally the profession had been far more flexible than that of *avocat.* The virtual exclusion of all but the *avocat* from litigation under the French legal system is not critical to legal practitioners because under the Napoleonic legal system the rule of law is typically formalized in codes and not determined, as in Anglo-American law, through court-litigated decisions. In addition, *conseils juridiques* in recent years have been allowed to represent clients in the *Conseil des Prud'hommes*, the lower commerce court.

Under the *conseil juridique* status, business lawyers, including foreign business lawyers, are allowed to give advice on a wide array of topics—tax, labor, investment, antitrust, merger, and so forth—and both French and foreign business lawyers may advise on either French or foreign law if educational and training requirements are met. These include a four-year college degree equivalency with a specialization in law and at least three years of practice, including a minimum of eighteen months in France under the supervision of an accredited *conseil juridique*. These requirements are similar for both French and foreign *conseils juridiques* and are not regarded as particularly stringent. (For example, they may allow a graduate from a business school to undergo an accelerated course of legal education and then enter the *conseil juridique* profession.) In addition, France along with the United Kingdom, but unlike the United States, Japan, or other major countries, is one of the very few countries that allow foreign lawyers to advise on local law unrestricted.

Conseils juridiques are allowed to associate with others to form a *conseil juridique* firm. This includes the right of non-French lawyers to associate with French *conseils juridiques*. While the new law put more restrictions on who might be able to become a *conseil juridique* and, more importantly, on who could start a new *conseil juridique* firm in the future, existing firms were protected under a grandfather clause. In effect, not much was changed under the new law except for the requirement that the countries of origin of the foreign *conseils juridiques* were to extend reciprocity within five years of the introduction of the 1971 law (which obviously excluded EC member states) or face the possibility that the Council of Ministers *might* adopt a decree limiting their practice principally to foreign and international law and excluding them from the practice of French law. The United States, and New York State in particular, were of special interest to French practitioners, and the measures taken by the New York legislature in 1974 (spelled out below) would seem to have fulfilled the rather loosely defined reciprocity requirements as they concerned U.S. law firms.

The United States

During the 1970s, two major steps toward liberalization were taken by the United States.[3] Under the 1973 *Griffiths* decision, the U.S. Supreme Court ruled that a qualified foreigner could not be excluded from legal practice by the states solely on the grounds of citizenship. Thereafter, a small number of foreigners received accreditation from various state bars. For example, half a dozen French lawyers now work for Paris-based international *avocat* firms with dual accreditation by the New York bar and the Paris bar. Such accreditation, however, is costly. It requires that individuals who have originally been accredited in their home country spend several additional years in a U.S. law school learning the American legal curriculum before they can acquire accreditation from a state bar.

Feeling under some pressure from the French, several large New York City law firms undertook in the early 1970s to convince the New York legislature of the need to respond to the French request for reciprocity expressed in the 1971 French law on the legal professions. To the relatively parochial upstate New York legal community, the proposal to create a professional status of "legal consultant" for foreign lawyers was presented as a way to promote the development of New York State and the New York state courts as centers of international legal activity. In 1974 the New York legislature and the New York Court of Appeals allowed the creation of a new "trained legal consultant" profession. This status permits qualified foreign lawyers to act as licensed legal consultants with the right to give legal advice freely on both their own legal system and so-called international law, and on New York state law and U.S. federal law "based on advice received from a member of the New York bar." While French authorities have argued that the new status is not quite comparable to the French *conseil juridique* status, because the ability of French lawyers to advise on U.S. law remains restricted, to date the issue has not been pressed any further.

Other countries complain, however, that except for New York State, the U.S. legal field remains closed to foreigners. Above and beyond the somewhat meaningless requests for

reciprocity from the fifty states and the District of Columbia—
which have been used at times as part of a negotiating tactic
rather than as a serious request—what foreign lawyers really
desire is access to a small number of key states in addition to New
York. At a minimum, the list includes Illinois, California, Texas,
and the District of Columbia.[4] This situation has been described
as follows in the recent OTA report:

> Pending proposals in the District of Columbia and Hawaii
> would create similar guidelines for the licensing of foreign
> attorneys, but a recently adopted Michigan rule, and a
> pending proposal in California, prohibit foreign attorneys
> from advising on State or Federal law, although permitting
> consulting on the laws of their own countries. Similarly, the
> Illinois Supreme Court recently rejected a petition that
> would have permitted foreign legal consultants to offer
> advice on U.S. and Illinois law.[5]

It has been argued on the other hand that access to New York
City, the world's financial and commercial capital and a premier
international legal center, provides ample evidence of the reciprocity afforded by the United States, and that thus far only a few
foreign lawyers have made use of New York's legal consultant
status to enter the market.

United Kingdom

The British legal profession is divided into the two well-
known specialties, "barrister" and "solicitor," with barristers
holding a monopoly on litigation except for a few situations in
which solicitors can also intervene.[6] Solicitors have a monopoly
on conveyancing and other services similar to those rendered by
the French *notaire*.

As is the case with American lawyers, the majority of
solicitors are small-scale, independent professionals; only a
minority are organized into large, multinational law firms
specializing in business law. The recent growth within British

firms of in-house counsels who do the basic work while farming out the more specialized work to outside law firms parallels a trend that occurred earlier in the United States.

Although citizenship has never been a requirement for barristers and has recently been removed for solicitors, foreign lawyers cannot act as barristers or solicitors and cannot hire or be hired by barristers or—except under very strict limitations—by solicitors. It is possible, but not practical, for an American lawyer to attempt to qualify as either a barrister or solicitor; for while an American law degree is given the equivalence of a British diploma in law, there are onerous requirements for further study, examinations, and a clerkship period, part of which is unpaid.

The foreign lawyer who wishes to practice in the United Kingdom is subject to the laws regulating the entrance and employment of aliens. A permit must be obtained from the Home Office after proof is offered of fitness qualifications and assurances are given to abide by British standards of conduct. Foreign lawyers may act as "legal consultants" in areas involving their native law or international law and may prepare the accompanying legal documents. With the exception of probate work and the preparation of conveyancing documents, they are also allowed to advise on British law. While there are many American and other foreign law firms in London, they have tended to be small and function mainly as referral sources for their clients.

West Germany

Foreign legal presence in West Germany is extremely restricted, largely because of the severe limitations imposed on independent practitioners, both foreign and domestic.[7]

The German legal system shares two similarities with its American counterpart. First, it is based on a unitary professional structure with the lawyer (*Rechtsanwalt*) providing a full range of services and possessing, since 1935, a monopoly on litigation. Second, it is based on a highly decentralized regulatory structure that operates primarily at the local level. Individual German lawyers receive regional accreditation and may not plead in more than one regional area. German law firms are restricted from associating with other firms in other regions. Such regulation has kept German law firms small and has encouraged German corporations, particularly the large international banks, to develop large in-house legal departments.

In West Germany, a lawyer requires both German citizenship and German training, with no equivalence recognized between German and foreign legal training. With the exception of pre-World War II German emigrés, foreign lawyers are not permitted to open an office in West Germany. To serve German clients, foreign lawyers, typically based in Paris or London, will operate on a transient basis—out of hotel rooms or by sharing physical space with German lawyers. Either arrangement is of dubious legality.

A point of entry for foreign lawyers might be provided by the statutory category of "licensed legal consultant" (*Rechtsbeistand*). The *Rechtsbeistand* must demonstrate professional competence but is not required to be a German citizen. A foreign lawyer would be limited to consultation on his native law and international law and would be limited in geographical scope to the district of the admitting court. Although there have been recommendations to upgrade the status of the *Rechtsbeistand* to a level generally comparable to that of the French *conseils juridiques*, to date the status of this profession has been kept low, making it unattractive as a vehicle for foreign lawyers to practice in West Germany.

Belgium

Until 1964, Brussels ran a close second to Paris in its openness to foreign lawyers. It offered some of the same advantages—including location, the opportunity to practice freely afforded by the unregulated profession of *conseiller juridique* (unencumbered by citizenship requirements), and the additional attraction of being the site of both the EEC and NATO headquarters.[8]

The influx of American firms in the 1960s, however, induced sufficient resentment on the part of the Brussels bar to lead to restrictive regulations. These included the need to obtain work permits, which were limited to ten in number and were issued on an individual, not a firm, basis. Further, legal services by foreign *conseillers juridiques* were to be provided only to foreigners and businesses in which foreign capital predominated. The number of American lawyers permitted to practice there was also to stay commensurate with the level of American investment in Belgium.

Subsequent protests by the U.S. State Department resulted in either the elimination of some of these regulations or the considerable softening of others. Brussels retains a slightly more restrictive environment than Paris, however, if only because the attitude of the local legal establishment is predominantly protectionist. To work with the Brussels bar requires the hiring of Belgian lawyers, but the same bar puts pressure on native lawyers not to work with foreign lawyers.

From a strictly Belgian point of view, however, the largely unregulated *conseiller juridique* profession has provided a vehicle for some unusual combinations since, as we noted previously, some of the large accounting firms in Belgium have been able to run *conseiller juridique* departments within their firms.

Other European Countries

Despite the convenience of its location, the presence of international organizations, and the presence of international arbitration institutions in both Geneva and Zurich, there are no foreign lawyers permanently established in Switzerland.[9] Foreign lawyers may engage in the activities of legal counseling and may represent clients before arbitration tribunals on a strictly temporary basis. A stay of up to eight days within any three-month period is the legal permissible maximum. Although in practice some leeway is afforded in the length of stay if there is no evidence of abuse of this privilege, authorization for a permanent or even an extended stay is extremely rare.

Other European countries to which foreign lawyers have been attracted include the Netherlands, where the maritime courts play an important role, and Sweden, to which the USSR—having rejected the Paris-based International Chamber of Commerce (ICC) arbitration system—has taken East-West trade arbitration cases.

Some foreign law firms have established offices in Stockholm, as a few foreign lawyers have done in the Netherlands—including the Japanese who, according to one lawyer, are using the Netherlands as one of their major platforms from which to enter the EEC.

Hong Kong and Singapore

For a number of reasons, Hong Kong has emerged as the major legal center in the Far East.[10] Its court system, which is part of the British court system, has a strong tradition of quality. The colony is a major financial center for the Pacific area and also plays a major role in maritime litigation, a field dominated by British law. The revitalized link to the People's Republic of China has increased its attractiveness to foreign lawyers, who are also interested in a grandfathered status before the termination of the Hong Kong lease arrangement.

British lawyers and other members of the Commonwealth are automatically admitted into the Hong Kong legal system. In 1977 the Law Society of Hong Kong invited other foreign lawyers to practice under legal counsel status, but limited this practice to advice on non–Hong Kong law.

Singapore provides the usual example of a domestic banking sector becoming increasingly internationalized and forcing an opening to foreign law firms despite the opposition of local lawyers. After independence in 1963, no foreign law firms were granted entry to practice. In the early 1970s, a handful of American firms were permitted to operate on an offshore trial basis, but only one of these had been permitted to remain by mid-decade.

By the late 1970s, however, Singapore bankers realized that an infusion of foreign legal talent was essential if Singapore was to compete with Hong Kong and capture a portion of the burgeoning offshore Eurocurrency banking business. Once Singapore's banking establishment convinced the Monetary Authority of Singapore that the local legal talent did not have sufficient expertise, the Authority successfully petitioned the attorney general's office to permit the entry of foreign law firms. The majority of respondents were London and New York law firms.

On the ground that Singapore law is based on British law, one London law firm petitioned successfully for admission to the local bar without going through the required examination process. The resulting protest from the local bar made this case the only exception thus far to the examination requirement. Foreign firms approved for practice are restricted to offshore financial work and are not allowed to practice Singapore law.

Japan

The modern Japanese attitude toward the entry of foreign lawyers has oscillated from relatively open entry before 1933 to restriction during the period of military buildup before World War II, from renewed openness in the first decade of postwar Allied occupation to the closing of the door again after 1955. Today Japan seems poised once more for some degree of openness.[11]

Although the Japanese legal profession has several categories of practitioner, the *bengoshi*, who has the exclusive right to engage in courtroom proceedings, is the best known because of the notorious difficulties of attaining that status. While every year nearly 25,000 graduates of Japanese law schools take the national examination, which is the prerequisite for entry into the Legal Training and Research Institute of the Supreme Court (the equivalent of the American bar), usually fewer than 2 percent pass this test and go on to take the two-year training course that will prepare them to become barristers, prosecutors, and judges. It is considered virtually impossible for foreigners, including those with a knowledge of Japanese, to negotiate these hurdles. A further difficulty is posed by the fact that since the fortunate few receive government stipends, a requirement of citizenship is imposed. Law school graduates who are noncertified are most likely to work in the in-house legal departments of large firms or for the government.

Between 1949 and 1955, perhaps ninety foreign lawyers, mainly Americans, obtained licenses without examination as special members of the Japanese bar advising only on foreign law. The disarray of the Japanese economy at the time prompted no substantial interest by Americans in further increasing their presence in Japan. After 1955, foreign lawyers were restricted to the position of "trainee" in Japanese law firms or of corporate legal counsel in Japanese corporations. In effect, foreign lawyers were restricted to advising on their home country law and on international law.

The subsequent large volume of American investment in Japan and the rise of Japan as a major international financial center stirred the interest of a few Japanese *bengoshi* in developing expertise in international business law by interning abroad with American law firms—and revived the interest of American law firms in establishing a presence in Japan. Subsequently, the Japanese government prevented the entry of foreign law firms by refusing to issue either visas or the proper licenses for this purpose. In 1977 the "foreign lawyer problem" was created when the government granted permission to a partner of Milbank, Tweed, Hadly and McCloy—Japanese-raised Isaac Shapiro—to open a law office in Tokyo. The ensuing vigorous protest of the Japanese bar led to the freeze on visas for foreign lawyers wishing to open offices in Tokyo as well as for those who wished to consult with Japanese clients. The counterprotest of the American government against a visa policy aimed at preventing the right of establishment has led to almost a decade's worth of reports, studies, and proposals.

In May 1986, the Japanese Diet passed the Foreign Lawyers' Practice Bill—expected to become effective in 1987—which would allow foreign lawyers to practice on a limited basis in Japan if reciprocity is maintained. In the case of the United States reciprocity is "defined as 'several states'." While foreign law firms will be able to establish offices in Japan, practice in Japan by foreign lawyers will remain restricted to home country law, international law, and laws of a third country if certain qualifications are met. Forming partnerships with or hiring Japanese lawyers will remain forbidden. The requirement that foreign lawyers—including those currently in Japan in a trainee status—have five years of experience in their own country would seem particularly onerous for those lawyers currently working as trainees since they lack such experience and would have to leave Japan for several years.[12]

The current thinking, however, is that the Japanese are unlikely to enforce this provision. Japanese law firms are small (staffs number ten to twelve, on average) and are frequently understaffed because of the small number of *bengoshi*. Those involved in international work are often critically dependent on both foreign trainees at home and links with overseas firms to carry out assignments. An out-migration of the foreign trainees would not be in the best interests of those firms.

THE REGULATION OF ACCOUNTING PRACTICE

Accounting, like other licensed industries, operates under national regulations that define the scope of operations of firms and determine entry of foreign individuals. Unlike legal services, however, solid, up-to-date, and factual information on the regulation by individual countries of the right of establishment and the right of practice of accountants is hard to come by. The most extensive source is a reference volume, *Professional Accounting in 30 Countries*, prepared by the American Institute of Certified Public Accountants (AICPA) and completed in 1975.[13] AICPA is revising the volume, but only information for three countries has been brought up to date at this writing. In addition, the original volume is usually quite specific regarding requirements on the right of practice but often vague concerning requirements on the right of establishment.

In this chapter, we summarize some of the information presented for fifteen key countries in this 1975 reference volume. While we have attempted to update that information as much as possible, in most cases we do not feel as confident about the accuracy of more recent information as we do with that provided twelve years ago by the AICPA.

In most countries today, the accounting profession is divided into two subprofessions: the public accountant, or bookkeeper, and the certified public accountant (CPA) or auditor. Public accountants usually keep books and prepare tax returns for firms and individuals alike. For the most part, their practice deals with small and medium-sized firms that choose to contract out such work. In continental Europe, such practice tends to be extensive; elsewhere it is somewhat more limited. The public accountant in the United States, the *expert comptable* in France, the *contador* in Argentina, Brazil, Chile, and Mexico, the *Buchhalter* in Switzerland, the *Vereidigte Buchprüfer* in West Germany, the *keirishi* in Japan—all are examples of this type of accountant.

Problems of foreign access for multinational accounting firms relate mostly, however, to the role of the certified public accountant in conducting the independent audits of public corporations required by United States and British law and, increasingly, the law of other nations as well. Both the British "chartered accountant" and the U.S. CPA (created on the British model) have set the standards for audit practice, which in other countries has been until recently a more diffuse and less regulated profession.

Our review of regulations of auditors and audit firms in fifteen countries, grouped by major regions, reveals a varying pattern of restrictiveness. What this review would seem to suggest is that, in many instances, the greatest restrictions are likely to be those on the right of establishment—including both the right to form audit firms or partnerships and the scope of services that can be provided under such establishments—rather than on the right of individuals to practice. Unfortunately, it is in this very area that information is most lacking. Our review also suggests that using bureaucratic red tape, including holding up visas, refusing educational or training equivalencies, holding up the right to form audit corporations for no apparent reasons, and other practices, is a popular device to restrict entry.

The United States

In the United States, licensing of individuals is regulated by the individual states. The general rule is that practitioners must, at a minimum, have a four-year college degree in accounting, pass a qualifying examination, and have two or more years of training. Half the states, including New York, have no ban on foreign practitioners but require that they indicate the name of the country in which they were certified whenever they issue accounting statements in this country. The other states, however, have either citizenship and/or residency requirements or require passing the state CPA examination.

EEC Member Countries

The United Kingdom, the Netherlands, and West Germany. As is the case in the United States, a certified accountant in the United Kingdom (chartered accountant), the Netherlands (*Registeraccountant*), and West Germany (*Wirtschaftsprüfer*) must have a degree from an institution of higher education, pass a qualifying examination, and have several years of experience in the field. West Germany requires six years of experience, making the average age of entry at least thirty.

There is relative ease of entry into these three countries, however: into the United Kingdom, where authorization is granted to qualified foreigners by the Ministry of Trade and Industry; into West Germany, where foreigners may practice if reciprocity between countries is observed; and into the Netherlands, where foreign accountants, after receiving revocable permission based on proof of competence acquired abroad, can receive authorization by the Ministry of Economic Affairs to carry out audits.

France. The independent public auditor did not occupy a significant place on the French scene until the mid- and late 1970s, when various reforms were introduced in the French accounting industry, in part to comply with EEC directives.[14] This was also true in most other southern European nations, where requirements for certification of accounts remained limited, if not nonexistent.

Until the early 1970s, the French *expert comptable* needed to obtain an appropriate accounting diploma (roughly two years after high school), pass a series of examinations, write a thesis, and acquire three years of practical experience. If reciprocity prevailed, the foreigner with acceptable qualifications could enter practice.

The then loosely defined audit function was divided between the *expert comptable* and the *commissaire aux comptes* (statutory examiner). The latter was appointed by a firm's shareholders and was expected to report to them about the financial statements prepared by the board of directors. An accounting diploma and two years of experience were required for inscription of a *commissaire aux comptes* on the official register, requirements that were less stringent than those for the *expert comptable* and weaker than those of a U.S. or U.K. practitioner.

During the 1970s, however, the role of the *commissaire aux comptes*, or *reviseur*, was made independent of a firm's board of directors, and the once relatively secondary activity of *revision comptable* became the more advanced of the two professions. Today requirements have been raised, and one must already be an *expert comptable* to become a *commissaire aux comptes*.

For nearly half a century, large British and American international accounting firms had no difficulty in operating offices in France. In the mid-1970s, however, as French accounting firms turned more and more towards certification of accounts, there was a new zealousness in enforcing previously unobserved rules. Foreign accountants were required to take oral examinations, and foreign firms were required to conform to French standards, including registration with the French professional accounting societies.[15]

The situation would appear to have changed again during the 1980s, as most of the large French audit firms, which had strived in the 1970s to remain independent, joined the large multinational affiliations one after another. (See Chapter 6.)

Belgium. The evolution of accounting in Belgium is not unlike the French experience. Until the mid-1970s, both public accounting and audit practices were in a fairly rudimentary state of development. *Experts comptables* had to either pass an examination or hold an equivalent college degree and have five years' experience under supervision. *Commissaires reviseurs* (statutory examiners) needed neither an accounting background nor Belgian citizenship. Most examiners were unregulated, except for a smaller specialized group of better educated examiners who were either bank auditors or corporate auditors and were nominated, respectively, by the Belgium Banking Commission and the Institut des Reviseurs d'Entreprises.

Today, as in other EEC countries, the distinction between *expert comptable* and *reviseur* has been formalized in the direction of upgrading and considerably tightening the licensing requirements for the *reviseurs*.

Italy and Spain. As has already been noted in Chapter 3, Italy and Spain represent, for all practical purposes, relatively new markets for certified audits: Italy, since the introduction of the EEC directives of the late 1970s and early 1980s, and Spain, since that country joined the Common Market. Subsidiaries of Swiss "accounting and fiduciary" firms (see below) as well as branch offices of the Big Eight moved aggressively into Italy early on. Both groups of firms come under the supervision of the Ministry of Industry and Commerce.

Switzerland. The Swiss auditing profession was subject to far fewer formal controls in the 1970s than was true in the United States. Originally, anyone could act, within limits, as an auditor, regardless of professional qualification. Increasingly, however, business firms are hiring certified auditors employed by regulated audit firms. Traditionally, the Schweizerische Treuhand- und

Revisionskammer (Chamber of Trustees and Accountants) has overseen the regulated part of the industry, including both professionals and firms: the certified accountants who carry out audits (to be distinguished from the certified bookkeepers); the fiduciary and accounting firms (the equivalent of American or British audit firms); and the bank auditing firms (a special group of fiduciary and accounting firms authorized to carry out bank audits).

Certified accountants must pass a qualifying examination, have three years of experience in the field, and have reached a minimum age of twenty-seven. The fiduciary and accounting firms are generally incorporated and have a legally required minimum capital. They are allowed to offer a wide range of services, such as statutory audits (including bank audits in the case of bank auditing firms), bookkeeping and accounting, preparation and filing of tax returns, tax consulting, management consulting, legal counseling, acting as trustees, and formal management of companies. Many fiduciary and accounting firms have traditionally been owned by the banks.

Latin American Countries

Brazil. An *auditor independente* is required to have a degree from an institution of higher education or its equivalent, pass a qualifying exam (unless the candidate already holds a specialized university degree), and have several years of experience in the field.

Brazil has no legal restrictions on practice by foreign accounting firms as overt as those contained in Venezuela's 1973 Public Accounting Law, which banned foreign firms altogether. But the evidence on Brazil's restrictiveness is ambiguous. In 1976 the U.S. Department of Commerce reported that, "in practice, the professional requirements imposed upon American firms are so onerous that only accountants possessing the requisite professional degree from a Brazilian university may practice within the country."[16] On the other hand, the fact that in 1979 local practitioners were denouncing the dominance of multinational accounting firms would seem to indicate that the barriers decried by the Department of Commerce had not proven impenetrable.

Argentina. The national public accountant (CPN) degree is conferred after completion of a five-year, specialized university curriculum, which in the accounting courses generally follows U.S. principles. In certifying the accounts of a corporation, the CPN, if subject to the jurisdiction of the Buenos Aires Stock Exchange, must follow certain internationally accepted standards of practice.

Chile. With a long history of resident British and U.S. accounting firms, accounting standards in Chile reflect Anglo-American practice. While not rigorously enforced, auditing standards are also similar. There are a number of qualified accountants engaged in auditing (*contadores profesionales auditores*). Even the statutory auditor (account inspector) is expected to be an accountant or a professional auditor.

Mexico. The public accountant (CP) must be a Mexican national, complete a five-year course, pass the qualifying examination, and defend a thesis. Certain sizes and types of businesses are legally required to have a CP certify their financial statements; auditing standards are virtually identical with those of the United States. The individual auditor signing the report is legally responsible for its contents, regardless of the type of firm that employs him.

Asian and Pacific Area Countries

Australia. As might be expected, Australia operates very much on the British model. There is relative ease of entry for qualified foreigners. Permission is usually granted to members of recognized foreign accounting organizations.

Japan. Registration as a foreign CPA is permitted in Japan if foreign qualifications are equivalent to the Japanese and the foreigner passes an examination on Japanese laws of accounting.

Japanese restrictions on the size and structure of the firm are difficult, however, for foreigners to negotiate. The audit firm (*kansa hojin*) must have five or more CPAs as partners, each with unlimited liability. Bureaucratic barriers to classification as a registered CPA can create interminable delays for foreigners who wish to form an audit firm.

India. Restrictions on the size of the accounting firm may also be used in India to impede foreign entry. The number of articled clerks a chartered accountant may hire varies according to previous years of practice—from one clerk for three years of practice to six after fifteen years. This requirement may impose severe restrictions on large foreign firms seeking to establish multioffice organizations in India.

CONCLUSIONS

Our brief review of the regulation of legal and accounting practices in key countries suggests that there are important issues relating to the right of individuals to practice and the right of individuals and/or firms to establish offices that underlie the liberalization of trade in professional services.

In the legal services, the major issues remain centered around the definition of the right to practice. De facto or de jure, all countries restrict considerably—if they do not simply prohibit—access by foreigners to the local bar. That restriction in itself, however, usually does not represent an overwhelming obstacle since a great deal of legal work everywhere involves the preparation of documents, not just litigation. Contentious issues, then, revolve mostly around restrictions that countries may place on who is allowed to carry out nonlitigation-related legal work and on which laws such individuals are allowed to advise—home country law, international law, or local law. Because of the way in which international law expertise is offered, a dozen or so countries at most are involved in this controversy. It would appear that countries such as France, Belgium, Singapore, the United Kingdom, and the colony of Hong Kong, have been and often remain among the most liberal, having made room for foreign legal consultants to enter and advise, more or less, on all three areas of law. By comparison, Japan and the United States would appear to have been among the most protectionist. For a long time both prohibited any type of practice by foreign legal consultants. The fact that non-U.S. citizens can now become lawyers accredited to a U.S. state bar does not constitute a realistic alternative for most. New York State and Japan have now introduced provisions for foreign legal consultants, but since in neither place are these legal consultants allowed to freely advise on local law, their capacity to serve their clients may be seriously curtailed. We remain cautious in formulating these generalizations because we found that even lawyers cannot agree among themselves on the extent of the restrictions that various countries place on the practice or entry of foreign legal consultants.

In accounting, it would seem that most countries are fairly liberal in granting foreign auditors the right to practice as residents, permission being based on partial or total equivalency for diploma and work experience acquired abroad. By comparison to the legal services, however—wherein the right of opening an office usually seems easy to obtain once one has been granted the right to practice—it seems that restrictions in accounting come mostly in the form of restricting the right of establishment, be it the number and size of the offices that firms can open or the scope of activity that they can carry out. Scope of activity is seen as a particularly important issue in mature markets, where accountants see diversification as the primary means to expand their businesses. Here, however, better information is needed before passing judgement. For example, while it may be true that a number of European countries have attempted to restrict the scope of business of some of the largest multinational accounting firms, such restriction has been difficult to implement because the national affiliates of these firms are typically set up as local partnerships or locally owned corporations. Furthermore, many European countries traditionally seem to have been far less restrictive than the United States in allowing accountants to offer a wide range of professional services, including not only tax and management consulting but also legal counsel. This is the case at least in France, Belgium, and Switzerland, where accounting firms are allowed to employ *conseils juridiques*, and in West Germany, where accounting firms are even allowed to employ fully qualified lawyers. It is worth noting, however, that the bar associations of both the District of Columbia and the state of North Dakota have taken steps recently to loosen up the traditional ban on partnerships among lawyers and other professionals.[17]

NOTES

1. For major sources of information on all countries reviewed here, see Kelly C. Crabb, "Providing Legal Services in Foreign Countries: Making Room for the American Attorney," *Columbia Law Review* 83, no. 7 (November 1983), John C. Hoppe and Zachary Snow, "International Legal Practice—Restrictions on the Migrant Attorney," *Harvard International Law Journal* 15 (1974).

2. For information on France's legal system and its governmental actions and legislation, see Christopher R. Brown, "France's Growing International Law Firms," *International Financial Law Review* (January 1984); Sydney M. Cone, III, "Foreign Lawyers in France and New York," *International Lawyer* 9, no. 3 (July 1975); "Loi No. 71–1130 sur la Reforme des Professions Judiciares et Juridiques," *Journal Officiel*, 31 Dec. 1971; "Circulaire du 16 Octobre 1972 relative aux Conseils Juridiques," *Journal Officiel*, 25 Oct. 1972, especially "Dispositions applicables aux personnes physiques et morales de nationalité étrangère"; Sydney M. Cone, III, "Government Trade Policy and the Professional Regulation of Foreign Lawyers," *University of Chicago Legal Forum* 1, no. 1 (November 1986).

3. For more information, see Cone, "Foreign Lawyers in France and New York"; Crabb, "Providing Legal Services"; Hoppe and Snow, "International Legal Practice"; see also "Foreign Attorney's Practice in Japan, Other Services Issues Focus of Chicago Conference," *International Trade Reporter* 13, no. 10 (February 12, 1986).

4. "Foreign Attorney's Practice in Japan."

5. OTA, *Trade in Services*, p. 83.

6. See Crabb, "Providing Legal Services," and Hoppe and Snow, "International Legal Practice."

7. Ibid.; see also Brown, "Europe's Top Lawyers and Law Firms."

8. Ibid.

9. Ibid.

10. See Crabb, "Providing Legal Services," and Hoppe and Snow, "International Legal Practice"; see also Margaret Thomas, "The Leading Euromarket Law Firms in Hong Kong and Singapore," *International Financial Law Review* (June 1983).

11. "Foreign Attorney's Practice in Japan"; Crabbe, "Providing Legal Services," and Hoppe and Snow, "International Legal Practice"; see also James S. Altschul, "Japan's Elite Law Firms," *International Financial Law Review* (June 1984).

12. *The Japan Times*, 17 May 1986.

13. The American Institute of Certified Public Accountants, *Professional Accounting in Thirty Countries*, New York: AICPA (1975).

14. See, for example, Coopers & Lybrand, *The EEC Directives* (Coopers & Lybrand Europe, 1984).

15. Edwin W. Macrae, "Impediments to a Free International Market in Accounting and the Effects on International Accounting Firms," in John C. Burton, ed., *The International World of Accounting: Challenges and Opportunities*, 1980 Proceedings of the Arthur Young Professors' Roundtable (Reston, Va.: The Council of Arthur Young Professors, Reston International Center, 1981).

16. John W. Buckley and Peter R. O'Sullivan, "International Economics and Multinational Accounting Firms," in Burton, ed., *International World of Accounting*, p. 117.

17. "Soon Anybody May Be Able to Own a Law Firm," *Business Week*, January 26, 1987.

6

ISSUES UNDERLYING TRADE IN BUSINESS SERVICES

In the 1983 *U.S. National Study on Trade in the Services,* the Office of the U.S. Trade Representative identified three major issues likely to be at the center of future negotiations on liberalizing international trade in the services:

1. The difficulty in distinguishing between pure trade and investment trade

2. The importance of immigration policy and professional licensing issues

3. The structure of competition in both domestic and international markets[1]

Based on what has been learned from this study of four business services, it may be useful to review how much new light can be shed on these issues.

DISTINGUISHING PURE TRADE FROM INVESTMENT TRADE

During most of the early postwar period, governments found it useful, when dealing with trade issues, to emphasize the distinction between pure trade (transborder trade) and investment trade (establishment trade) and to seek liberalized regional or multilateral regulatory regimes for transborder trade while letting investment trade issues fall under national sovereignty. The dominance of goods trade in the early postwar economy and the relative ease with which goods produced locally and those produced abroad could be distinguished made such an approach all the more appropriate. The remaining critical issue in most trade negotiations at the time concerned the securing of equal access for foreign goods to local distribution networks so that, once import duties had been paid, they would not suffer discrimination. Under the General Agreement on Tariffs and Trade (GATT), *access* to local distribution networks by foreign producers through distribution and maintenance service contracts came to be regarded as a trade issue, but *upfront ownership* of a local distribution system, as an investment issue.[2]

Today a major problem confronting negotiators is the extent to which a similar formulation can be developed to address trade in services. The authors of the *U.S. National Study*, while emphasizing that advances in computerized technology were enhancing the "tradability" of services, were nevertheless careful in recognizing that a formulation similar to that developed for goods might not be possible.

We agree with the authors of the *U.S. National Study* and would further argue that there might be dangers in overemphasizing the potentials for increasing tradability of services, for two reasons. First, stressing tradability in the services results in part from a misinterpretation of both *technological* trends and *market* trends. Second, opportunities for transborder trade in business services are likely to remain highly restricted because of the desire by countries to regulate service providers, especially in the case of the licensed professions. We review these two important points in this and the next section.

Clearly, advances in computerization and communications technologies are making it increasingly feasible to design service production procedures in the form of software and to store inputs and outputs in electronic memories, so that the production of services can increasingly be separated from their consumption, both in time and in space. In that sense, the new technology has powerful centralizing potentials that may enhance the tradability of services. The error, however, would be to see in the computerization of services no more than the industrialization of service production and to assume that services are becoming more and more like goods, that the bulk of their value can increasingly be created in a centralized location, and that the importance of distribution matters only to the extent that access to distribution can be used as a barrier between producers and consumers.

Such interpretation is not uncommon and is based largely on what we would regard as the "misinterpreted" case of the financial service industries. According to the conventional wisdom, financial products can now be produced in one country and sold in another simply by establishing data communication linkages between financial service producers and local distribution networks. What such interpretation implicitly assumes is that the computerization of production has made it possible to remove much of the production of the value added away from the distribution network. And that is simply wrong.

Indeed, what our own studies of computerization in the service industries indicate is that, in effect, the new computerized communications technologies create a dual centralizing-decentralizing tendency.[3] On the one hand, the potential for centralization made possible by computerization may be particularly attractive when major scale economies are involved or when part of the value of a service originates from the very process of large-scale data integration (for example, in securities trading systems or cash management systems). On the other hand, not all data bases need to be centralized. This is true especially in light of the fact that sharp drops in the cost of computerized technology has made distributed data processing systems highly attractive alternatives to centralized ones, from both an investment and an operating cost point of view. For instance, neither a U.S. bank operating a cash management system for European middle-market firms nor a consumer banking business in Latin America needs to do its processing out of New York or Chicago. Furthermore, the computerization of routine production procedures enhances the capacity to customize the output. In turn, much of this customization can only be done close to the market, that is, as part of the relationship between the distributor and the final consumer. In other words, the computerization of production processes helps to generate new opportunities for creating new value added in the distribution/customization process. And in today's economy, this customization capacity may very well be emerging as the most important prerequisite to staying competitive.

These are fundamental dimensions of the service economy. The current wave of computerization is not about the industrialization/mass production of services in the same sense that assembly line production revolutionized manufacturing. If anything, the service economy is evolving toward greater market segmentation and further customization of outputs (of *both* goods and services) than in the past, and this evolution is being reinforced by the new technology. That trend acts as a powerful decentralizing force.[4]

Several of our interviews with accounting professionals point strongly to this pull-push tendency in their sector. In one case, for example, improved communications linkages had already made it possible for the firm to open "mini-branch" offices staffed only with accountants and project managers, not with partners. While only partners have the right to sign off on statutory audits, the firm had relied for several years on telex communications and was in the process of upgrading that system to a more sophisticated electronic mail system through which project managers could relay relevant information from the branches to the partners located in the central offices. In the opinion of the executive interviewed, this was opening new opportunities for the firm to get closer to its clients out in the field. In addition to being in a better position to customize their services, accounting firms like to be near their clients because they must deal with the great variety of computer systems used by those clients. Under such conditions, it typically makes more sense for accountants and project managers to run audit checks directly on the *client's* computer systems, on the client's premises, not on their firm's own computer systems.

While some large law firms emphasize computerization and centralization of paralegal work to enhance the production of certain legal documents, a great deal of the value added in this sector also originates in the identification and delivery of the service in the field—based on relationships between the senior lawyer and the associates, the lawyer and the client, the lawyer and the courts, and so forth. One can hardly see how this is likely to change in the near future.[5]

In compensation work—an area of management consulting that has grown tremendously during the seventies and eighties—the introduction of computerized technology has not only made it easier for firms to rationalize the way they perform the actuarial work involved in designing a pension plan or a compensation plan, but also to penetrate further and deeper into their market hinterland. Increasingly, as with other services, a key to expanded business is customization of plans. Also, given the nature of the output, clients (typically, personnel managers) will often prefer to discuss issues involved in the preparation of such plans away from their own offices, where they may risk being overheard. Computerization facilitates customization, which in turn strengthens, rather than weakens, the role of the local branch office. Not surprisingly, management consulting firms that specialize in compensation work have extensive branch office networks.

Another reason for paying more attention to the local investment issue is the tendency for business service firms to seek new business opportunities in the corporate middle market and among certain segments of the consumer market. Typically, developing such opportunities will call for building a strong local presence.

These findings have broad applicability to other services. In a tabulation presented in the OTA report cited in Chapter 2 and reproduced here as Table 6–1, OTA shows the ratio of U.S. direct service exports to total foreign revenues for twenty-two service sectors.[6] This table shows that the twenty-two sectors can be divided into three distinct groups: (1) those for which direct exports account for 95 percent or more of total foreign revenues (travel, franchising, licensing, education, and legal services); (2) those for which direct export represents between 40 and 61 percent of total foreign revenues (health, transportation, construction, information, telecommunications, motion pictures, miscellaneous, management and consulting, and software); and (3) those for which direct export represents 25 percent or less of foreign revenues (engineering, insurance, data process-

Table 6–1.   Ratio of U.S. Direct Service Exports to Total Foreign Service Revenues, 1983.

Travel	1.00[a]
Franchising	1.00[a]
Licensing	1.00[a]
Education	0.98
Legal	0.95
Health	0.61
Transportation	0.61
Construction	0.61
Information	0.50
Telecommunications	0.50
Motion pictures	0.50
Miscellaneous	0.47
Management/consulting	0.45
Software	0.40
Engineering	0.25
Insurance	0.22
Data processing	0.17
Investment banking/brokerage	0.16
Advertising	0.15
Leasing	0.14
Accounting	0.08
Retailing	0.00
Total	0.42

Source: U.S. Congress, Office of Technology Assessment, *Trade in Services: Exports and Foreign Revenues*, Special Report OTA-ITE-316 (Washington, September 1986), p. 43. See Table 2–6.

a. Direct export totals equal foreign revenue totals by definition.

ing, investment banking and brokerage, advertising, leasing, accounting, and retailing). The first group constitutes approximately 30 percent of all service exports; the second, 50 percent; and the third, 20 percent. (See Table 2–5 in Chapter 2.) In foreign revenue terms, the first group constitutes approximately 14 percent; the second, 43 percent; and the third, 43 percent (see Table 2–6 in Chapter 2).

A possible conclusion would be that those service industries that do most of their business through affiliates are likely to contribute little to the U.S. balance of payments and to domestic jobs, while those that export services in substantial volume will contribute much more directly to the nation's economy. Our analysis, however, suggests a different conclusion, for three major reasons. The first is that the demand from foreign affiliates is itself a cause for exports. OTA's own estimate is that $7.2 billion of the $75.4 billion worth of service exports in 1983 were exports to U.S. service affiliates abroad (the difference between all exports and direct exports, as shown in Tables 2–5 and 2–6 in Chapter 2). Since OTA could capture only the intrafirm exports of insurance and investment banking, because of measurement problems, this figure is most likely an underestimation. The second reason, shown earlier, is that in many service sectors, including the four sectors reviewed in this book, the firm's ability to serve clients domestically is increasingly linked to its ability to serve them abroad, whether or not cross-border flows of services are involved. In other words, growth in domestic markets is partly linked to growth in foreign markets. The third reason is that at a time when markets are increasingly organized by customer segments (for example, small firms, large firms, hospitals, banks, affluent consumers, and so forth) rather than by regions or countries, the ability of firms to develop markets that are large enough to be profitable may be increasingly linked to their capacity to operate across national borders.

In sum, a conceptual separation between pure trade and investment trade in services may not only be extremely difficult to establish, but simply wrong from a policy point of view. Some investment issues need to be discussed as part of a trade regime for the services. In practice, this has already been done in the Declaration on Service Trade appended to the U.S.-Israeli Free Trade Agreement of 1985. We return to this issue in Chapter 7.

IMMIGRATION POLICY AND PROFESSIONAL LICENSING ISSUES

The need to bring investment issues into trade negotiations does not exhaust all sources of difficulty. Another reason why a pure trade regime is probably not applicable to negotiations for the services is the critical importance of labor mobility and professional licensing issues in those sectors.

Trade in professional services assumes that a service produced by a licensed professional from one country (or someone under his or her authority) can be sold to residents of another country in which the professional is not originally licensed to practice. Most countries, including the United States, have traditionally regulated such activities rigorously.

Countries have argued that it is their duty to designate who is licensed to offer a service and who is not so that they can protect their consumers by controlling the integrity of those who render services. Because of the difficulties inherent in assessing the qualifications of professionals educated and trained abroad, countries often set a minimum residency requirement before they will qualify foreign professionals to practice in the local market. While such provisions can be and have been used to discriminate against foreign service providers, it is obvious that national regulation does serve a wider purpose. Still, by linking the right to practice to residency, most countries have created a de facto link between professional trade and immigration policy issues.

Clearly, accounting and legal services are only two examples from a long list of professions that are subject to similar constraints: physicians, nurses, veterinarians, dentists, psychologists, teachers, insurance brokers, stock brokers, real estate brokers, engineers, architects, and so forth. Still, the link between trade and immigration policy is obviously not forged solely by the need for licensing in the professional services. As Peter Drucker noted in a 1986 *Wall Street Journal* editorial, developing an international company in today's economy means projecting a transnational image.[7] Increasingly, multinational companies are trying to transcend local or national markets and are focusing on consumer segments—on either a world scale or, at the very least, a multinational scale. To a very large extent, this means developing procedures for producing and marketing goods and services on a global instead of local, market segment basis. In turn, such a capacity requires being able to move personnel around because, in the services, transferring "technology" is largely about transferring "training." Drucker notes that a few multinational corporations—Citicorp, IBM, and others—already do that extensively, and gives the example of Citicorp's U.S. credit card operation headquartered in North Dakota but managed by a Venezuelan. Our own recent research on banks and insurance companies suggests that this ability to develop a cadre of multinational managers is becoming a critical issue among internationalized firms, be they Japanese, French, Swedish, or American.[8] A similar concern was voiced by large accounting and advertising firms in the course of our interviews. Staffing a foreign affiliate with nonlocal personnel raises the issue of national sovereignty over who is allowed to work in a given country. Most countries place some form of control, usually via the issuance of visas and work permits, over the number of foreigners that can staff a foreign affiliate.

The experience of the European Community (EC) in addressing the issue of licensing and trade in professional services is illuminating. Under the terms of the Rome Treaty, all restrictions on trade by citizens of member states were presumably lifted within the EC. But once the issue of freeing trade in professional services surfaced in the 1970s, the EC discovered that it had to deal with a set of barriers not addressed in the treaty: national restrictions on professional licensing.

In the mid-1970s, several decisions by the European Court reaffirmed the applicability of various articles of the Rome Treaty to the professions as well as the power of EC legislation to overrule national restrictions. Thereafter, the EC followed a two-track approach in dealing with the problem. In its short-term approach, the EC focused on developing rules that would permit professionals of one member country to practice in another member country. With the exception of lawyers—for whom early efforts had been made to enable them to practice in another member country on a *transient* basis—the emphasis for most professions was on eliminating restrictions that limited the rights of professionals in EC countries to practice as *residents*. The EC's longer term approach is to lift restrictions on the right of professionals to practice on both a resident *and* a transient basis. That approach involves bringing different licensing requirements among member states into parity through standardization of university curricula and postgraduate training requirements and, when needed, standardization of professional rules. In its efforts toward harmonizing licensing regulations, the EC has made major advances in the medical, nursing, veterinarian, midwife, dental, and accounting fields. In terms of the harmonization of accounting standards, the EC adopted several directives, including Directives No. 4 and No. 7, that order member states to enact national laws bringing their accounting standards in line with each other. Most of the key member states have already enacted these laws.[9] Restrictions on lawyers remain the most stringent, although the EC now has provisions allowing *avocats* from one member state to represent clients in the courts of another member state on a transient basis.[10]

The EC experience—which involves countries with a much higher level of commitment to economic integration than can be expected from almost any other trade forum—should serve as a useful reminder of a few simple truths. Harmonization of professional standards and standardization of licensing requirements are not only desirable but a prerequisite to transborder trade in professional services. But long and difficult negotiations are necessary to achieve such harmonization and standardization. In a multilateral setting broader than that of the EC, given the legitimate concern of nations for regulating professions and controlling immigration, at first one should only expect to focus on liberalizing trade on a resident basis. There might be exceptions, such as accounting, where a previous history of multilateral negotiations through international professional bodies might make it possible to address issues of transient trade readily.[11] In the short term, however, such exceptions are likely to be few.

COMPETITION IN DOMESTIC AND INTERNATIONAL MARKETS

A third key issue raised by the authors of the *U.S. National Study* was that of competition.[12] Their concern was that problems of competition in sectors either dominated by publicly owned monopolies or characterized by regulated environments would need to be addressed in service trade negotiations. Only the latter situation applies to the four sectors examined in this book.

Broadly speaking, we would argue that a fundamental dimension of growth and economic development in the service economy is the increased availability of expertise and specialized knowledge in business service firms, which both existing and start-up businesses can draw on to expand rapidly.[13] This represents a fundamental change from the industrial period, when firms had to rely on the slower and more costly process of creating and developing the in-house expertise needed for growth. In the new environment, the network of business services becomes part of the infrastructure upon which economic growth can be built.

The implicit conclusion is that the more extensive the network of business services, the better off a country should be. If we assume further that preserving competition is the best way to ensure continued high levels of development, countries may want to prevent either of the following scenarios from occurring:

- A particular sector reaches a high level of development, but becomes characterized by rapid concentration—with the inherent risks of oligopolistic pricing and growing disincentives for new technological developments within the sector.

- A particular sector is largely underdeveloped, yet becomes dominated by just a few firms, either domestic or foreign, that have few incentives for technology transfers or for extensive development of local resources.

However, based on limited market-share data presented below, we would conclude that most business service markets are and will remain quite competitive in the years ahead, even though there is growing concentration in a number of subsectors.

Advertising

In advertising, available data point to mixed tendencies. While a very large share of the world market is held today by multinational advertising firms, thus far most large national markets remain characterized by the continued presence of a relatively large number of firms and high degrees of competition. In smaller markets—typically those of less developed economies—there would appear to be greater concentration.

The fact that advertising must continue to play on national and local cultural differences would seem to ensure that decentralization remains necessary, at least in the development of effective local campaigns. Nevertheless, the trend toward global advertising works in favor of developing advertising concepts and strategies in a limited number of centralized locations, while leaving the responsibility for the relatively more mundane tasks of developing operational campaigns to local agencies. In that respect, a critical issue for most countries is, of course, that many of the world agencies are from the United States, meaning that global advertising concepts and strategies tend to be developed on Madison Avenue, not elsewhere.

These mixed tendencies are revealed in Table 6–2, which is derived from *Advertising Age*'s agency revenue data for twenty-eight countries in 1985. The table shows the market share of the five top-ranking agencies in each country for 1985 (measured by share of revenues); the country rank of each of the twelve largest world agencies (eleven U.S. firms plus Saatchi & Saatchi, Compton—a U.K agency); and the number of these twelve world agencies that rank among the top ten agencies in each of the twenty-eight countries. The twenty-eight countries are organized into four groups: eleven West European countries, six Latin American countries, Canada, and ten Pacific area countries. For market shares of the top five agencies in each country, Table 6–2 shows average shares of 38.3 percent in Western Europe and 36.6 percent in Canada, but markedly higher ones for Latin America and the Pacific area—56.3 and 58.1 percent respectively.

Table 6–2 shows that the twelve world agencies occupy more than half of the top ten spots in six of the eleven West

European countries, four of the six Latin American countries, and seven of the ten Pacific area countries. Typically, countries with a minimal presence of these large firms are those that have made efforts to limit their influence: France and Sweden in Western Europe, Brazil in Latin America, Japan and South Korea in the Pacific area.

With this mixed record in mind, a number of countries are likely to be worried about the future impact of the current rash of mergers, which can be expected to concentrate still further an enormous amount of billing power within a few world agencies (see Table 6–3). Saatchi & Saatchi estimates that today 20 percent of world advertising billing is controlled by the eight largest advertising firms, compared to 12 percent by the twelve largest agencies ten years ago.[14] Undoubtedly, with the formation of the new Saatchi & Saatchi and the new BBDO, Doyle, Dane & Needham (both following in the footsteps of the reconstituted Interpublic Group of Companies), a fundamental, qualitative change has now taken place. In the past, the rule was that no advertising firm could control more than one worldwide network of agencies because conflicts of interest in handling more than one firm in a given industry would lead to client defections. Put more simply, this rule meant that the existence of, say, twenty major multinational food companies ensured the preservation of approximately twenty competing multinational advertising firms. Yet Saatchi & Saatchi, BBDO, and Interpublic are now attempting to run more than one worldwide network of agencies under the same roof: Saatchi & Saatchi, Compton and Ted Bates for Saatchi & Saatchi; BBDO International and DDB Needham Worldwide for BBDO; and McCann Erikson Worldwide, SSC&B-Lintas Worldwide, and Marschalk Campbell Ewald Worldwide for Interpublic.[15] While the rest of the industry was quick to criticize these strategies when the Saatchi & Saatchi and BBDO mergers were first put together in early 1986, there are indications that the basic concept may be working. If so, the potentials for new, similar mergers are great, in part because gains from scale economies, economies of scope, and increased market power can be enormous.

Table 6–2. Structure of Advertising Market in Twenty-Eight Countries, 1985.

	Market Share: Top 5 Agencies Share of Advertising Revenues	Individual Country Rank of the Twelve Largest					
		Young & Rubicam	J. Walter Thompson	McCann Erickson	Ogilvy & Mather	Leo Burnett	Ted Bates
Austria	45.8%	6	10	3	5	—	18
Great Britain	32.3	8	2	6	5	19	12
France	45.0	5	16	18	15	35	23
West Germany	33.5	7	4	3	5	12	16
Greece	48.8	—	1	10	—	3	5
Italy	32.5	5	2	1	9	22	25
Netherlands	29.4	4	10	12	1	8	26
Norway	56.7	5	15	7	4	—	1
Spain	30.7	15	1	6	11	20	3
Sweden	43.5	6	20	19	14	—	1
Switzerland	32.2	5	19	1	11	17	—
Average[a]	38.3						
Argentina	49.5	14	1	8	4	11	18
Brazil	52.2	13	6	9	7	17	—
Chile	58.4	9	1	2	8	18	11
Colombia	62.4	—	3	4	7	1	6
Mexico	52.3	8	4	2	6	7	—
Venezuela	75.8	9	1	3	2	4	—
Average[a]	56.3						
Canada	36.6	6	2	9	5	14	15
Australia	42.0	8	11	6	3	10	1
Hong Kong	48.8	4	6	5	1	2	3
India	58.0	—	1	—	4	—	3
Japan	74.3	17	13	7	29	22	25
Malaysia	54.2	9	3	8	1	7	2
New Zealand	54.6	—	9	5	7	10	—
Singapore	48.3	5	7	2	1	3	9
Thailand	68.3	15	8	4	2	5	3
South Korea	80.4	—	8	—	—	—	—
Taiwan	n.a.	—	1	—	—	5	—
Average[a]	58.1						

Source: "Agency Income Report," Advertising Age, April 21, 1986.

Note: This table makes no distinction between a wholly owned subsidiary, a joint venture, or any other legal arrangement that an agency may have with a host nation. It shows how selected agencies rank by gross income within the national advertising industry.

a. Unweighted modified average for the group.

b. Out of nine firms.

c. In Taiwan, out of a total of six agencies listed by Advertising Age.

U.S.–U.K. World Agencies

BBDO	SSC&B Lintas	Foote Cone & Belding	D'Arcy McManus	Grey Advertising	Saatchi & Saatchi, Compton	Number of 12 Largest Agencies Among Top 10
9	4	17	14	15	7	7
29	20	15	4	9	1	7
27	12	19	24	26	6	2
1	2	26	27	6	8	8
4	7	11	15	—	8	7
6	—	30	24	19	8	6
2	7	17	14	24	5	7
—	11	12	3	16	14	5
4	2	35	21	24	16	5
11	17	21	18	2	16	3
6	8	—	26	27	13	4
6	16	10	17	5	—	6
16	15	22	—	—	14	3
3	5	—	—	7	—	7
2	—	11	—	8	5	8
12	21	20	13	17	19	5
—	—	5	—	8	7	8[b]
8	29	17	18	16	13	5
2	12	14	7	19	16	7
22	11	10	18	9	7	9
5	2	—	—	—	8	6
6	—	30	24	19	8	3
10	6	—	—	—	4	9
1	11	12	6	13	3	7
8	11	12	16	6	13	8
11	1	—	—	9	12	7
5	—	—	—	6	3	4
4	—	—	—	2	3	5[c]

A careful reading of the list of the top forty or so world advertising firms, including the top fourteen presented in Table 6–3, indicates that, with the exception of Saatchi & Saatchi (originally a British firm), only a few Japanese and French firms have succeeded in maintaining some standing, largely because of the rather protective domestic environments within which they have been able to operate. These include: Number Five, Dentsu;

Table 6–3. The Fourteen Largest Advertising Agency Groups Following Rash of 1986 Mergers, by 1985 Billing ($ billions).

Rank	Firm	Billings
1	Saatchi & Saatchi Saatchi & Saatchi, Compton; Dancer Fitzgerald Sample; Baker Spielvogel; Ted Bates[a]	7,800
2	BBDO, Doyle, Dane & Needham BBDO Intl; Doyle Dane Bernbach group; Needham Harper Worldwide[a]	5,040
3	Interpublic Group of Companies[b]	4,600
4	Young & Rubicam	3,620
5	Dentsu Inc.	3,580
6	Ogilvy Group	3,320
7	J. Walter Thompson	3,010
8	Foote, Cone & Belding Communications Foote, Cone; Leber Katz Parkers[a]	2,180
9	D'Arcy McManus Masius D'Arcy McManus; Benton & Bowles[a]	2,120
10	Leo Burnett	1,870
11	Grey Advertising Grey Advertising; Levine, Huntley, Schmidt & Bearer	1,730
12	Hakuhodo Intl	1,530
13	Bozell, Jacobs, Kenyon & Eckhardt Bozell & Jacobs; Kenyon & Eckhardt[a]	1,220
14	Eurocom Group	866

Source: Advertising Age as quoted in *Business Week*, May 12, 1986.

a. All are 1986 mergers. Billings are estimated on the basis of the 1985 billings of agencies prior to the mergers.

b. Parent of McCann Erikson Worldwide, SSC&B-Lintas Worldwide, and Marschalk Campbell Ewald Worldwide.

Number Twelve, Hakuhodo International; Number Twenty-Six, Dai Ichi Kihachi; Number Twenty-Eight, Daiko Advertising; Number Thirty, Tokyo Advertising, all the foregoing in Japan; Number Sixteen, Eurocom International; Number Twenty-Three, Publicis Intermarco Farmer; Number Twenty-Five, Havas Conseil/Martsteller; Number Thirty-Four, TBWA; and Number Thirty-Five, Roux, Seguela, Cayzac et Goudard, all from France.[16] By comparison, the United Kingdom, with a far more liberal policy, saw most of the U.K.-based firms taken over by Madison

Avenue during the 1960s and early 1970s, although this clearly did not stop the emergence of the largest firm in the world today, Saatchi & Saatchi (more on this below).

The French and Japanese records are likely to be used by some countries to argue that some degree of control over competition in their domestic markets can be helpful in maintaining strong, homegrown advertising industries. These countries will argue that they need to ensure that the development of the industry contributes as much as possible to the development of their local human resources; that resources specifically associated with the development of world advertising concepts be developed domestically, because of the linkages to other services (noted in Chapter 3) such as market research, strategic planning, and product planning; and that strong linkages be developed between the local advertising industry and the video/television/media industry in order to foster the latter's development. But these arguments will need to be weighed against the fact that the Japanese and French firms, while domestic giants, have turned out to be rather weak international players, often unable to serve their countries' largest firms adequately as they moved increasingly into foreign markets.

Law

In the field of international business law, the evidence is also mixed. In the United States, the past ten years have seen the buildup of so-called mega-firms, be it through internal growth or through mergers.[17] The reasons, again, are economies of scale and scope. Nevertheless, the long-range impact of the trend remains difficult to assess in a field that is often atomistic and still rather competitive. From the point of view of other countries, however, the U.S. market for business legal services remains overwhelmingly dominated by U.S. firms, despite the narrow opening provided by New York State's legal consultant status for some foreign legal professionals.

Likewise, the U.K. evidence would seem to suggest a similar, overwhelming predominance of U.K. solicitor firms in London.

While numerous there, foreign law firms would appear to remain at a major competitive disadvantage in doing sizable business in the city. As was noted earlier, we suspect that, in both the United States and the United Kingdom, the long-established connections of local lawyers to key U.S. and U.K. financial intermediaries remain a major factor in their comparative advantage.

Elsewhere, the evidence would seem to suggest the existence of more competitive markets for legal services. In France, for example, the arrival of U.S. firms in the 1950s and 1960s did much to spur activity and competition in a field that previously had been stagnant. At first it inspired others—both French and non-French—to start their own *conseil juridique* firms. And in the mid- and late 1970s, the renewed competition motivated a new generation of French *avocats* to start their own *cabinets d'avocats*, specializing in international business (Table 6–4).[18]

By comparison, protectionism by the West Germans may have retarded the development of their own legal sector. Aside from the in-house legal departments of the three large German banks, which may employ over 100 lawyers each, strong independent business law firms have been rare until recently. Only over the past five to ten years have a few independent German law firms with some market clout emerged.[19]

In both Hong Kong and Singapore, as was noted earlier, the opening of legal service markets appears to have allowed for healthy competition among firms from various countries, although U.S. and U.K. firms often play the major roles. In Hong Kong, there are now about twenty U.K. firms and thirteen other foreign firms competing with local firms. Singapore now has at least eighteen foreign law firms. (See Table 6–5 for major foreign law firms in these two markets.)

The question mark, of course, is Tokyo, which thus far has remained relatively protectionist. (See Table 6–6 for major international law firms in Japan.)

In the long run, the evolution of the legal market is likely to be determined in part by changes in the traditional bank–law firm relationships. Today's transformation of capital markets on a world scale is bringing about the emergence of an upper tier of banks—both commercial and investment, and dominated by

Table 6–4. Leading Independent *Conseils Juridiques*, Foreign *Conseils Juridiques*, and International *Avocat* Firms in Paris, 1983.

Firm	Founded	Partners	Associates
Independent *Conseils Juridiques*			
Law Offices of S.G. Archibald	1907	13	25
Phillips & Giraud	1977	4	2
Salans, Hertzfeld, Heilbronn, Beardsley & van Riel	1977	7	5
Foreign *Conseils Juridiques*			
Coudert Frères	1879	11	29
Cleary, Gottlieb, Steen & Hamilton	1949	9	18
White & Case	1959	2	3
Clifford Turner	1962	12	14
Davis, Polk & Wardwell	1962	2	5
Shearman & Sterling	1963	6	6
Rogers & Wells	1965	3	3
Surrey & Morse	1970	3	6
International *Avocat* Firms			
Gide Loyrette Nouel	1920	20	48
Jeantet	1925	10	15
Monahan & Duhot	1960	6	2
J.C. Goldsmith & Associes	1967	2	2
Tandeau de Marsac, Serrero, Popineau & Associes	1971	5	3
Giroux, Buhaghiar & Associes	1973	7	9
Simeon Moquet Borde & Associes	1974	4	16
Chartier, Hourcade, Weiser, Jobard, Guillerm-Kirk	1975	5	3
Berlioz Ferry David Lutz & Rochefort	1978	6	13
De Pardieu & Associes	1982	1	5
Delvolve & Associes	1983	4	5

Source: Christopher R. Brown, "France's Growing International Law Firms," *International Financial Law Review* (January 1984): 5.

Note: This list is not exhaustive, simply indicative.

perhaps a dozen U.S. institutions, half a dozen British institutions, half a dozen Japanese financial firms, and only a few

Table 6–5. Leading Foreign Business Law Firms in Hong Kong and Singapore, 1982.

	Country
Hong Kong	
Coward Chance	UK
Herbert Smith & Co.	UK
Linklaters & Paines	UK
McKenna & Co.	UK
Norton, Rose, Botterell & Roche	UK
Simmons & Simmons	UK
Sinclair, Roche & Temperley	UK
Slaughter & May	UK
Stephenson Harwood	UK
Coudert Brothers	US
Milbank, Tweed, Hadley & McCloy	US
Cleary, Gottlieb, Steen & Hamilton	US
Shearman & Sterling	US
Simpson, Thacher & Bartlett	US
White & Case	US
Singapore	
Coudert Brothers	US
Graham & James	US
Simpson, Thacher & Bartlett	US
Baker & McKenzie	US
Sidley & Austin	US
White & Case	US
Norton, Rose, Botterell & Roche	UK
Freshfields	UK
Sinclair, Roche & Temperley	UK
McKenna & Co.	UK
Wilde Sapte	UK
Clifford Turner	UK
Coward Chance	UK

Source: Margaret Thomas, "The Leading Euromarket Law Firms in Hong Kong and Singapore," *International Financial Law Review* (June 1983): 4–8.

others—with enormous influence in the three key financial markets—New York, London, and Tokyo.[20] An important question in terms of the international legal service market is whether or not this transformation of capital markets may lead to the

Table 6–6. Leading International Law Firms in Japan, 1984.

Firm	When Founded	1984 Partners	1984 Associates
Adachi, Henderson, Miyatake & Fujita	1974	6	3
Blakemore & Mitsuki	1949	9	2
Braun, Moriya, Hoashi & Kubota	1954	8	4
Hamada & Matsumoto	1972	4	4
Komatsu & Tomotsune	1967	9	7
Logan, Okamoto & Takashima	1949	6	4
Masuda & Ejiri	1977	4	5
Matsuo & Kosugi	1963	3	7
McIvor, Kauffman & Christensen	1914	6	5
Milbank, Tweed, Hadley & McCloy	1977	2	2
Nagashima & Ohno	1961	10	14
Nakagawa Law Office	1976	2	7
Nishimura & Sanada	1964	6	16
Tanaka & Takahashi	1952	5	4
Tokyo Aoyama Law Office	1966	4	12
Welty, Shimeall & Kasari	1948	3	6
Yagi, Fukushima & Yamanouchi	1972	3	8
Yuasa & Hara	1902	26	20

Source: James S. Altschul, "Japan's Elite Law Firm," *International Financial Law Review* (June 1984): 9.

formation of a tightly knit, and rather exclusive, set of relationships between those few financial institutions and a few law firms from the United States, the United Kingdom, and even perhaps Japan. Another intriguing question is whether or not we might soon see large law firms, in New York and London for instance, attempting to link up through the merger of partnerships as a way to strengthen and expand their reach.

Accounting

Data on the accounting sector suggests rather high degrees of market power in areas of service most directly targeted to the multinationals, but a continuing high degree of competition in the expanding market for medium-sized corporate customers.

Historical data for a few countries gathered by Bavishi and Wyman in *Who Audits the World* point to the increasing power of the Big 9 during the 1970s in the market for large corporate audits.[21] As shown in Table 6–7, there was strong market share concentration by the Big 9 in the United Kingdom, Canada, and Australia between 1971 and 1981, resulting in a dwindling market share for the small affiliations and nonaffiliated firms; down from 28 percent to 14 percent in the United Kingdom, 58 percent to 1 percent in Canada, and 68 percent to 29 percent in Australia. In the United States, the market was already highly concentrated by 1971.

Such data may still underemphasize the extent of concentration on both a regional and a functional basis. As shown in Table 6–8—based on data gathered by Daniels et al. for the United Kingdom—in the London area, four firms controlled nearly two-thirds of the fees raised by the nine largest firms in 1985, whereas in the West Midlands, one firm (Coopers & Lybrand) controlled one-fourth of the fees generated by the nine largest firms.[22] Bavishi and Wyman also present data that indicate a strong tendency toward specialization by functional areas (banks, hospitals, food companies, and so forth) among large accounting firms.[23]

While we were unable to locate historical or geographical data for other countries as detailed as the data presented in Tables 6–7 and 6–8, there is considerable evidence that similar processes

110

Table 6–7. Percentage of Certified Audits Conducted by Big 9 Accounting Firms, Small Affiliations, and Non-Affiliated Firms for a Sample of Large Corporations in the U.S., U.K., Canada, and Australia, 1971 and 1981.

	United States		United Kingdom		Canada		Australia	
	1971	1981	1971	1981	1971	1980	1971	1980
Big 9 firms	95.0	99.0	72.0	86.0	42.0	99.0	32.0	71.0
Small affiliations	1.0	0.0	8.0	5.0	41.0	0.0	12.0	3.0
Nonaffiliated firms	3.0	1.0	20.0	9.0	17.0	1.0	56.0	26.0
Total	100.0	100.0	100.0	100.0	100.0	100.0	100.0	100.0
Number of large corporations in sample	1,870	3,202	677	1,266	484	719	139	229

Source: Vinod B. Bavishi and Howard E. Wyman, *Who Audits the World; Trends in the Worldwide Accounting Profession* (Storrs, CT: University of Connecticut Center for Transnational Accounting and Financial Research, 1983), pp. 135, 137, 138, 139.

111

Table 6–8. Auditors Ranked by Fee Income in Two U.K. Regions, 1984 (in thousands of British pounds).

	Fee Income	Percentage
London area		
Ernst & Whinney	19,028	19.0
Deloitte Haskins & Sells	16,454	14.4
Coopers & Lybrand	15,629	15.6
Price Waterhouse	15,166	15.1
Peat Marwick	9,881	9.9
Klynveld Main Goerdder	8,351	8.3
Touche Ross	7,174	7.2
Arthur Andersen	4,315	4.3
Arthur Young	4,314	4.3
Total	100,312	100.0
West Midlands		
Coopers & Lybrand	3,931	25.5
Peat Marwick	2,570	16.6
Ernst & Whinney	2,021	13.1
Arthur Andersen	2,017	13.6
Price Waterhouse	1,334	8.6
Deloitte Haskins & Sells	1,323	8.6
Touche Ross	1,030	6.7
Klynveld Main Goerdder	711	4.6
Moore Stephens	505	3.3
Total	15,442	100.0

Source: Accounting Journal, 1985. In Peter Daniels, Andrew Leyhson, and Nigel Thrift, "U.K. Producer Services: The International Dimension" (Working paper, St. David's University College, Lampter, and University of Liverpool, August 1986): 19.

of concentration are under way elsewhere. Even in France, which, like Japan, had managed to maintain an independent domestic auditing industry until recently, the early 1980s saw large local auditors joining the largest international affiliations in droves. As shown in Table 6–9, today only two of the top fifteen French auditing agencies remain independent.

However, there is more to the accounting market than the audit of large companies by the largest affiliations. With regard to other segments of the accounting market, the evidence would seem to suggest continued intense competition for small and

Table 6–9.   Fifteen Largest French Accounting Firms with Specialization in Audit, Tax, and MAS, Fiscal Year 1985 (in millions of French francs).

Rank	Firm	Fees	Affiliate
1	Helios Streco Durand	197	Arthur Young
2	Guy Barbier & Associes	140	Arthur Andersen
3	DeBois Dieterle & Associes	120	Touche Ross
4	ACL Audit	110	Coopers & Lybrand
5	Blanchard Chauveau &Associes	100	Price Waterhouse
6	BEFEC	94	Binder Dijker Otte
7	Frinault Fiduciaire	89	Klynveld Main Goerdder
8	Audit Continental	70	Peat Marwick
9	SEEC-Reydel Blanchot	68	Dunwoody Robson
10	Cabinet R. Mazars	65	MSA Intl
11	Guerard Delbor Vallas	65	Unaffiliated
12	MONTEC	50	Ernst & Whinney
13	La Villeguerin Audit	50	Moores Rowland Intl
14	FIDULOR	50	Unaffiliated
15	PAREX	49	Deloitte Haskins & Sells

Source: "La Profession Comptable, " No. 27-28, 21 Feb. 1986, in Commissariat Général du Plan, Rapport du Groupe de Strategie Industrielle No. 9, Services aux Entreprises (Paris, 1986), pp. 190, 191.

medium-sized firms. In the United States, for example, a number of second-tier accounting firms have done rather well by focusing on niches within that expanding market. In France and other European countries, there is evidence that the old "monopoly" of the large *fiduciaires* in bookkeeping and accounting for small and medium-sized firms is being challenged by a number of new players: the Big 8 firms trying to penetrate the market; management consultants trying to sell not only straightforward accounting services but also financial management advice; and, a few data processing/software houses that have moved faster than the *fiduciaires* in offering computerized and now PC-based accounting products.

With regard to nonaccounting services, as we suggested in Chapter 3, audits have become a way to get clients for other, more profitable services such as tax or management advisory services. The power of the linkage between accounting and other services

Table 6–10.   Top Ten Management Consultants in the United States, 1985 ($ millions).

Firms	Consulting Revenues
Arthur Andersen, MAS	472
Towers, Perrin, Forster & Crosby	400
William Mercer (Marsh & McLennan)	235
Arthur D. Little	233
Peat, Marwick, Mitchell, MAS	224
Booz Allen & Hamilton	200 (est.)
McKinsey	200 (est.)
Ernst & Whinney, MAS	190
Price Waterhouse, MAS	173
Touche Ross, MAS	144
Hay Associates (Saatchi & Saatchi)	123

Source: Association of Management Consulting Firms, quoted in "Management Consultants," Economist, May 17, 1986.

is best demonstrated by what has happened in the management consulting industry in the United States after the mid-1960s, where the market share of the MAS divisions of the Big 8 grew from almost insignificant levels to nearly one-third of the market today.[24] Indeed, ACME's most recent tabulation of the leading management consultants shows that only four of the top ten firms remained independent (see Table 6–10). Nevertheless, management consulting is such a fast growing field that sizable room remains for smaller firms to grow.

Management Consulting

To conclude this review of competitive conditions, some additional points must be raised about management consulting. First, the growing linkage between management consulting and accounting is not limited to those two sectors. In a related field, there is evidence of a growing linkage between public relations firms and advertising firms. For example, Table 6–11 shows that in the New York area market, nine of the top fifteen public relations firms are now owned by advertising firms.

Table 6–11. Top Fifteen New York Public Relations Firms Ranked by N.Y. Employment.

Rank	Firm	Parent	Number of N.Y. Employees	Fees ($ millions) N.Y.	Worldwide
1	Burson-Marsteller	Young & Rubicam	750	46	110 (1985)
2	Hill & Knowlton	JWT Group	525	n.a.	120
3	Ruder Finn & Rotman	Independent	225	13	21
4	Doremus Porter Novelli	Omnicom Group	190	12	20
5	Ogilvy & Mather PR Group	Ogilvy & Mather	180	n.a.	30
6	Manning, Selvage & Lee	D'Arcy MacManus Masius	162	11	22
7	Howard J. Rubenstein Ass.	Independent	122	n.a.	n.a.
8	Rowland Saatchi Group	Saatchi & Saatchi	105	n.a.	21
9	D-A-Y Public Relations	Ogilvy & Mather	100	n.a.	n.a.
10	Daniel J. Edelman Inc.	Independent	90	6	23
11	Adams & Rinehart Inc.	Ogilvy & Mather	85	n.a.	n.a.
12	Bashe Communications Inc.	Independent	75	n.a.	n.a.
13	Dorf & Stanton Communications	Independent	75	4	5
14	Robert Marston & Assoc.	Independent	72	8	8
15	Greycom	Grey Advertising	70	4	4

Source: O'Dwyer's Directory of Public Relations Firms, as quoted in Crain's New York Business, Jan. 12, 1987.

Table 6–12. Fifteen Largest Management Consulting Firms in the United Kingdom, 1980, Ranked by Number of Professionals.

Rank	Firm	Number of Professionals
1	P.A. Management Consultants	501
2	Ibucon/AIC Management Consultants	350
3	Coopers & Lybrand Associates (Philadelphia)[a]	200
4	PE International	181
5	Peat Marwick Mitchell (New York)	135
6	Urwick, Orr & Partners	120
7	Arthur Andersen (New York)	107
8	Price Waterhouse Associates (New York)	86
9	Knight Wegenstein (Chicago)	82
10	McKinsey (New York)	74
11	Deloitte, Haskins & Sells Management Consultants (New York)	70
12	UIMC (Unilever)	60
13	The Economist Intelligence Unit Ltd.	55
14	Hay-MSL Ltd. (Philadelphia)	54
15	Stanford Research Institute (San Francisco)	50

Source: *Financial Times*, Jan. 29, 1980.

a. Coopers & Lybrand's MAS division is headquartered in Philadelphia, not New York.

Second, the growing influence of other business service firms in the management consulting field in the United States appears to be carrying over elsewhere. According to a 1980 survey by London's *Financial Times*, nine of the top fifteen management consulting firms in the United Kingdom at the time were affiliates of U.S. firms, including five affiliates of the Big 8 (see Table 6–12).

CONCLUSIONS

International trade in services raises a host of new problems, including the need to deal with issues of foreign direct investment, immigration, professional licensing, and market competition. In particular, the review conducted in this chapter suggests that negotiations on liberalizing trade in many business services will need to focus initially on liberalizing establishment trade—since labor remains the fundamental input of business services and since countries are unlikely to forfeit their rights to regulate the supply of business services to their markets by means of restrictions on transient trade. In addition, a quest for liberalized trade in business services will need to recognize that the negotiation process may contribute to raising major questions regarding the competitive structure of many business service markets.

In general, multinational business service firms will demand that they be able to expand their activities worldwide. In those countries that still place heavy restrictions on the geographical expansion of these multinationals, the firms are likely to place emphasis on expanding their basic network of local offices; in other countries, on expanding the scope of their activities and the range of their customers.

But some countries will want to make sure that they retain some control over the pace and direction of such expansion, if only to ensure the development of their own service economy infrastructure. Most will likely accept, however, that their chances of rapidly creating their own large multinational business service firms, capable of competing with those already established, are limited. In the near or medium term, the only country that might have the means to take exception with that statement is Japan. As has been pointed out, business services such as accounting and law are strongly linked to financial services and Japan could use the emergence of its financial institutions as major world players to foster the development of a few large accounting and legal firms of its own.

In choosing among policy options, countries will need to remember that overly restrictive policies vis-à-vis multinational business service firms will likely be counterproductive. Such policies will either deny large local firms access to the expertise that they need to compete in international markets or give them an incentive to acquire it abroad. In both cases, restrictive countries will simply lose opportunities for local employment and for training of natives in some of the most advanced business service practices and gain little in return. At a minimum, however, many countries are likely to be concerned with maximizing their return from the presence of large multinational business service firms or with ensuring the development of strong local industries to serve their medium-sized corporate markets and their consumer markets. Some of those concerns are likely to translate into attempts to retain spillover effects of some of those sectors—for example, in areas such as the production of advertising videos, human capital formation, and so forth. In the end, however, we would argue that there is much room everywhere for the expansion and creation of business service firms targeted at both corporate middle markets and some of the consumer markets, and that this should be an important element to recognize in any national policy geared toward business services.

NOTES

1. *U.S. National Study on Trade in the Services*, section 3, pp. 69–74.
2. Ibid., section 3, p. 71.
3. Olivier Bertrand and Thierry J. Noyelle, *Technology, Skills and Skill Formation in French, German, Japanese, Swedish and U.S. Banks and Insurance Companies*, Expert Report to the Center for Educational Research and Innovation of the Organization for Economic Co-Operation and Development (Paris: OECD, August 1986).
4. Eli Ginzberg, Thierry J. Noyelle, and Thomas M. Stanback, *Technology and Employment: Concepts and Clarifications* (Boulder, Colo.: Westview Press, 1986), especially ch. 1.
5. John Mollenkopf, *The Corporate Legal Service Industry*, Report to New York City's Office of Economic Development (New York: 1984).
6. OTA, *Trade in Services*, p. 43
7. Peter F. Drucker, "The Changing Multinational," *Wall Street Journal*, 15 Jan. 1986.
8. Bertrand and Noyelle, *Technology, Skills and Skill Formation*.
9. Coopers & Lybrand, *The EEC Directives*.

10. Council Directive of March 22, 1977 to facilitate the effective exercise by lawyers of freedom to provide services (77/249/EEC), *Office Journal of the European Communities* 20, no. L78 (March 26, 1977).

11. Rossi, "Government Impediments."

12. *U.S. National Study on Trade in Services*, section 3, p. 69.

13. Noyelle, "Economic Transformation."

14. Saatchi and Saatchi, *Fiscal Year 1986 Annual Report*, as reported in *New York Times*, 5 Dec. 1986, Business section.

15. While the formation of the Interpublic Group of Companies dates back to earlier days, for most of its existence the group was seen as a holding of largely unconnected agencies. It was not until 1982–83 that Interpublic attempted to consolidate several of its agencies to form its three much denser, but truly worldwide, networks.

16. *Advertising Age*, April 21, 1986.

17. "Mega Firms Are Taking Over Corporate Law," *Business Week*, November 17, 1986. See also, "New York Firms Learn Business Rules the Law," *Crain's New York Business*, November 10, 1986.

18. Christopher R. Brown, "France's Growing International Law Firms," *International Financial Law Review* (January 1984): 4–8.

19. Christopher R. Brown, "Europe's Top Lawyers and Law Firms," *International Financial Law Review* (October 1983): 4–7.

20. Thierry J. Noyelle, "New York City and the Emergence of Global Financial Markets," Report to the New York Regional Plan Association, November 1986.

21. Bavashi and Wyman, *Who Audits the World*, p. 144.

22. Daniels, et al., "U.K. Producer Services."

23. Bavashi and Wyman, *Who Audits the World*, pp. 141–42.

24. Noyelle, *The Coming of Age of Management Consulting*, p.32.

7

LESSONS FOR SERVICE TRADE NEGOTIATIONS

Strong emphasis was placed throughout this book on the fact that multilateral service trade negotiations will need to address issues linked to establishment trade, immigration policy, and licensing policy. Such an emphasis will assume a major departure from the approach followed in earlier multilateral trade negotiations, which focused on liberalizing transborder trade to the exclusion of other issues.

There is some historical precedent for dealing with investment and immigration issues within the framework of trade regimes, principally in bilateral friendship, commerce, and navigation treaties (FCN treaties), in multilateral sectoral agreements, and in Common Market treaties. Usually, however, these have required a level of shared commitment to change that goes far beyond that which can be expected in a large-scale multilateral setting. Nevertheless, in 1986 in Punta del Este, Uruguay, GATT members agreed to work together toward developing a multilateral agreement on trade in services.

The form that such an agreement is likely to take has yet to be negotiated. The U.S. position thus far has been to push for the formulation of an umbrella agreement covering all service sectors, complemented by sector-specific agreements or codes.

In this final chapter, we make no attempt to give a specific answer to this question of the form to be taken by a GATT agreement. Nevertheless, we attempt to identify some of the terms that are likely to be necessary in the formulation of a broad-based multinational trade regime in services—terms consistent with what has been learned here about trade in business services. We also present some suggestions on areas that may-need special attention in that part of the GATT negotiations that would focus on business services.

A WORKING PRINCIPLE FOR A MULTILATERAL REGIME: BALANCING OBLIGATIONS AND RIGHTS

Traditionally, multilateral trade regimes have tended to emphasize shared obligations and principles allowing liberalization of trade flows among nations without encroaching upon national sovereignty. In contrast, bilateral or sectoral agreements usually have tried to create much greater levels of commitment, necessitating some encroachment upon national sovereignty. Normally, this has been done by balancing liberalizing principles with better defined national rights. Any attempt at developing a mutlilateral liberalizing trade regime for services will probably require the latter approach.

This suggestion is not particularly original and has already been proposed by others. In a recent paper on trade liberalization, in which he focuses on the licensed professions, John Barton proposes several formulations to reconcile requirements for accepting foreign professionals with the legitimate immigration concerns of nations.[1] His suggestions revolve around the notion that a "nation might be required to accept up to a specific quota of professionals, perhaps a number agreed in advance, perhaps a number based on a formula involving population, GNP etc."[2]

In a similar vein, Karl Sauvant concludes in his recently published book, *International Transactions in Services*, that since transborder trade issues cannot be fully separated from establishment trade issues, any serious attempts at negotiating a liberalization of trade in services must also involve serious efforts at negotiating clearer foreign direct investment rules.[3] His specific suggestion is to put more emphasis on moving ahead with the negotiation of investment codes, including the code on transnationals being negotiated through the United Nations Center on Transnational Corporations.

In the following paragraphs, we propose our formulation of both multilateral obligations and country rights that may need to be spelled out in a multilateral service trade regime. Our suggestions and comments are not meant to be exhaustive. In considering our preliminary set of multilateral obligations, the reader should remember that since such obligations are *conditioned* by rights, they take their full meaning only once rights have been spelled out as well. We have assumed that negotiations should seek to define obligations that are as broad as possible from the outset, while much of the bargaining and concessions would focus on more specific definitions of rights. The definition of rights could be updated periodically as the internationalization of services proceeds further and as countries adjust to the impact of such internationalization.

MULTILATERAL OBLIGATIONS

Right of Establishment

Parties signatory to a multilateral service trade agreement would recognize a firm's right to an establishment presence and seek to ease such access. This right must be recognized especially if we are to deal with situations in which restrictions on the right of practice are such that market access through transborder trade is either very limited or very difficult and is likely to stay that way in the near future. This is the case not only in the licensed professions but also in the financial services, where specific local capital requirements may be imposed.

A possible precedent is the nonbinding declaration on service trade appended to the United States–Israel Free Trade Agreement of 1985 (dealing primarily with goods). The declaration includes the "right to a commercial presence," defined as "situations when a commercial presence within the nation is necessary to facilitate transport of a service from the other national or is required by that Party."[4] Earlier on, U.S. negotiators appeared to emphasize that this right was meant to cover "distribution" rather than "production" facilities. Their position seems to have changed somewhat recently. We would discourage this earlier emphasis since, in each of the four services studied here, the loci of production and distribution are often hardly distinguishable from each other and are unlikely to become any more distinguishable in the future than they are at the moment.

This right of establishment would be conditioned by national rights, such as the right of countries to impose capital requirements, conditions on the staffing of such establishments, and other reasonable requirements. (See below.)

Right of Practice

Parties to the agreement would extend a reasonable right of practice to individuals from other countries signatory to the agreement—meaning, a right of practice that does not put such individuals in a markedly disadvantageous competitive position. One objective of such an obligation would be to seek reasonable standardization in various countries of the right of practice and the right of entry of practicing individuals, subject to each nation's right to organize a particular industry or profession and to define its immigration policy.

In the case of legal services, for example, a principal objective of negotiations might be both to define a legal consultant or *conseil juridique* status that is comparable among those nations signing the agreement and to ease entry of such foreign professionals. The latter obligation, however, could be constrained by immigration policy goals or by competition policy concerns— including, perhaps, the right of countries to ensure that no more than a given percentage of practitioners in a given profession are foreigners.

National Treatment

In GATT, the national treatment principle is defined as follows:

The products of the territory of any contracting party imported into the territory of any other contracting party shall be accorded treatment no less favorable than that accorded to like products of national origin in respect of all laws, regulations and requirements affecting their internal sale, offering for sale, purchase, transportation, distribution or use.[5]

This concept will need to be reformulated from the ground up, not only because it will have to cover both transborder and establishment trade situations but because the right of nations to regulate certain activities to protect themselves and their consumers may create situations of somewhat less than perfect national treatment. For example, countries might need to impose higher capital requirements on foreign financial institutions than those imposed on domestic institutions. Some markets may also be closed to foreign practitioners on the grounds of national security.

Market Access

Parties to an agreement would agree to take steps to ease market access by foreign producers by easing transborder trade, the movement of individuals and professionals, the establishment of a commercial presence, or access to restricted market segments (for example, public-sector markets). While this easing of market access would be subject to better defined national rights, market access would likely constitute the principal focus of sector-specific codes or agreements (see next major section below).

Most-Favored-Nation Treatment

The principle of most-favored-nation (MFN) treatment provides that any market access or other commitment granted to any

125

one country that is party to a given agreement is granted to all other countries adhering to the same agreement.

If the negotiated service trade agreement turns out to involve both an umbrella agreement and a series of sector-specific agreements, MFN treatment would need to be made conditional by applying only to those that have signed each particular agreement.

When the reasonable number of available slots for foreign providers in any one country might be below the number of legitimate candidates, some auctioning mechanisms might need to be put in place to limit entry. This might be the case, for example, in the allocation of seats to foreign brokers on stock exchanges or in the allocation of bank audit status to foreign accounting firms in countries that separate bank auditing from enterprise auditing.

Transparency

Parties to the agreement would seek to clarify and identify for others the rules used to keep foreign competition out, be they de jure or, even more importantly, de facto. For that matter, the organization of fact-finding sectoral negotiations in most of the services studied here may be the most useful follow-up to a similar strategy begun with the November 1982 GATT call for national studies on trade in services.

COUNTRY RIGHTS

Economic Security

Negotiators should seek to establish reasonable rules allowing countries to regulate specific areas such as the right of establishment or the right of practice in ways that protect their consumers without, however, creating insurmountable comparative disadvantages. Examples of this would be rules defining the capital requirements of foreign affiliates or the liability of foreign professionals.

National Security

The agreement would recognize the existence of areas in which foreign firms or nations are not allowed to compete, on the grounds of national security. Countries could restrict to national firms activities such as the audit of sensitive public-sector agencies or the awarding of sensitive public-sector contracts (for example, redesigning the computer systems of the military command).

Immigration Policy

The agreement would recognize the right of countries to control their own immigration policy within limits that do not completely exclude foreign competitors. John Barton's suggestion of using negotiable entry quotas for resident foreign professionals seems reasonable.

Competition Policy and Economic Infrastructure

The agreement would recognize the right of countries to set the terms of competition in given markets, including the right to take steps to ensure the growth of the domestic sector, as long as the objectives are to foster the overall development of the sector and not to shut out foreign competitors completely. For example, if one of the objectives of negotiation was to ensure market access of foreign providers to certain government procurement markets in countries where domestic firms are still weak, access by foreign firms could conceivably be restricted to joint ventures between foreign firms and one or more domestic firms.

A SPECIAL FOCUS ON BUSINESS
SERVICES

Within the broad framework of an umbrella agreement, negotiations of sector-specific codes or agreements would likely focus principally on increasing market access. For business services, this would include improving market access to multinational clients wherever they need to be served; expanding access to local, domestic markets; and expanding access through a broadening of the firm's offering. Large multinational business service firms would probably be the most active in promoting these objectives. Since many of those are U.S. or U.K. firms, and often hold commanding leads in business service markets, trade negotiators from both countries may find that they will need to exercise great care in approaching future trade negotiations and in avoiding strategies too narrowly focused on demanding fewer impediments and ever bigger market shares.

The remarkable worldwide expansion of large business service firms over the past two to three decades hardly supports the notion that those firms have met with overwhelming protectionist conditions infringing on their ability to serve their traditional clients, namely, the large multinational firms. True, some countries did restrict access to some sectors. Nevertheless, more often than not, such practices evolved on an ad hoc basis— usually reflecting the specific, not to say parochial, interests of the local professionals rather than as part of a wider protectionist scheme. Thus, Germany might have been relatively restrictive with lawyers, but remained relatively free of major restrictions in advertising or accounting. France became protectionist in advertising, but remained far less so in accounting or legal services (despite repeated posturing to the contrary).

Large business service firms will argue, however, that conditions have changed in recent years. First, these firms have encountered relatively more restrictive environments in many of the newer, fast-growing Asian-Pacific markets. Second, an increasing number of countries have become concerned with the need to protect their emerging small and medium-sized corporate markets. In short, a growing number of countries have responded to their own perception of the rising importance of business services in a restrictive manner.

We think that broadening market access, especially when services are aimed at large or very large corporate customers, is in the best interest of all parties involved and constitutes a legitimate area for vigorous negotiation. In today's world economy, denying access to large business service firms is likely to be counterproductive, particularly to the very countries that do so. This is the case either because such policy ultimately denies large local corporations access to expertise that they need to compete in world markets or because these corporations will simply bypass local restrictions and purchase needed expertise abroad. As a result, restrictive countries deny themselves opportunities for local employment, output, and skill creation. In addition, as was noted in the case of the large French and Japanese advertising firms, while protecting business services markets may have helped create domestic giants, thus far it has rarely proven to be the best way to create national champions that are truly competitive on world markets.

Increasing market access to the emerging, mostly domestic, small and medium-sized corporate market will probably be a more contentious issue, because a number of countries are likely to see those markets as areas of opportunities in which to develop local expertise and entrepreneurship. While large multinational business service firms will argue that their greater access to this market will increase competition to the benefit of all, such claims will have to be balanced against the legitimate interest of countries to promote the growth of a local business service sector. In the interim, it must be noted that these markets are, and are likely to remain, a development primarily of the advanced countries, possibly also of the newly industrialized countries. In Western Europe those markets remain fairly open and, for that matter, may often be more accessible to new foreign entrants than are North American markets. Among Asian-Pacific and NIC countries, the picture seems more mixed.

Another growing market where liberalized access is likely to be sought by large business service firms is public-sector procurement. In contrast to the middle-sized corporate market, historically this market has been highly protected. Clearly a modicum of new competition can only serve the general economic welfare. Furthermore, earlier trade negotiations provide some precedence for opening up public-sector markets. This being said, a number of countries might argue legitimately that the size and sophistication of both the U.S. market and U.S. firms must be given due weight. In particular, simply opening U.S. public-sector procurement to foreign suppliers may represent a rather insignificant gain from the point of view of other countries, since foreign firms are often much smaller than their U.S. counterparts. Parties to the negotiations may want to develop formulas that encourage U.S. firms to set up joint ventures with foreign firms for the purpose of serving some of the large U.S. public-sector markets for accounting, software, consulting, legal, advertising, and other business services. Similarly, the United States might agree that, in some countries, freer access to public-procurement markets will be achieved primarily, at least at first, through joint ventures between U.S. and local firms. The United States might also encourage provisions for small business set-aside programs to alleviate fears of market domination by large, mostly U.S. firms. In short, this is an area where constructive concessions might be obtained from the United States, if only as a counterpoint to a basic agreement on greater openness of such markets.

Expanding market access through expanding the scope of activities individual business service firms are allowed to enter may be one area that many countries will view as falling within the domain of national sovereignty and, for all practical purposes, outside that of international trade negotiators. Nevertheless, a legitimate case can be made that international negotiations will have to determine the extent to which restrictions are applied equally to both domestic and foreign competitors and when applied selectively, whether restrictions to foreign firms serve a legitimate purpose or are fundamentally protectionist. Here it must be noted that the United States itself will need to make efforts to loosen its current regulatory framework that, for example, limits the ability of different professions to work together much more than is the case in West European countries.

In concluding, business services are sectors in which some useful steps could indeed be taken to bring about freer trade in ways that represent new opportunities and new challenges for all of the parties involved. As our analysis has shown, it would be incorrect to view a process of liberalization as yielding beneficial results only for the most advanced countries and/or the largest firms. Business services are among the fastest growing markets worldwide, with enormous opportunities both for old firms to expand and for new ones to emerge. In addition, freer trade in business services is unlikely ever to produce the employment displacement problems that, in some cases, have resulted from trade in goods. Finally, countries entering the business services markets later than others do have room to influence the process of market opening in ways that can enhance the development of their own market and of their domestic sector.

NOTES

1. John Barton, "Negotiation Patterns for Liberalizing International Trade in Professional Services," *University of Chicago Legal Forum* 1(1986).
2. Ibid.
3. Karl Sauvant, *International Transactions in Services: The Politics of Transborder Data Flows* (Boulder, Colo.: Westways Press, 1986).
4. Ibid, p. 183.
5. Article III.4 of GATT, as quoted in Barton, "Negotiation Patterns."

Index

ABOUT THE AUTHORS

Thierry Noyelle is a senior research scholar at the Conservation of Human Resources, Columbia University. He is the author and coauthor of several books, including *Services/The New Economy* (1981), *The Economic Transformation of American Cities* (1984), *Technology and Employment* (1986), *Beyond Industrial Dualism* (1987), and *Human Resources and Corporate Strategy: Technological Change in Banks and Insurance Companies in Five OECD Countries* (1988).

Anna B. Dutka is a senior research associate at the Conservation of Human Resources, Columbia University. She is the author of *New Types of Work Scheduling: The United States Experience* (1985) and coauthor of *Life After Early Retirement* (1983), *Training Information for Policy Guidance* (1980), *Work and Welfare in New York City* (1975), and other works.